Sight Unseen

Sight Unseen

An Exploration of Conscious and Unconscious Vision

Melvyn A. Goodale
University of Western Ontario,
Canada

and

A. David Milner
University of Durham,
UK

OXFORD
UNIVERSITY PRESS

OXFORD

UNIVERSITY PRESS

Great Clarendon Street, Oxford OX2 6DP

Oxford University Press is a department of the University of Oxford.
It furthers the University's objective of excellence in research, scholarship,
and education by publishing worldwide in

Oxford New York

Auckland Cape Town Dar es Salaam Hong Kong Karachi
Kuala Lumpur Madrid Melbourne Mexico City Nairobi
New Delhi Shanghai Taipei Toronto

With offices in

Argentina Austria Brazil Chile Czech Republic France Greece
Guatemala Hungary Italy Japan Poland Portugal Singapore
South Korea Switzerland Thailand Turkey Ukraine Vietnam

Oxford is a registered trade mark of Oxford University Press
in the UK and in certain other countries

Published in the United States
by Oxford University Press Inc., New York

© Goodale and Milner 2004, 2005

A catalogue record for this book is available from the British Library

Typeset by Newgen Imaging Systems (P) Ltd., Chennai, India
Printed in Great Britain
on acid-free paper by
Biddles Ltd., King's Lynn, Norfolk

ISBN 0–19–851052–7   978 0 19 851052 9 (Hbk.)
0–19–856807–X   978 0 19 856807 0 (Pbk.)

10 9 8 7 6 5 4

To Joan and Christine, for their forbearance and for being there.

PREFACE

The story of this book began over 30 years ago in St Andrews, Scotland, where the two authors met and first began to work together. It would not have been written, however, but for the events that unfolded some 15 years later than that, when the two remarkable people we are calling Dee and Carlo first entered our lives.

The fortuitous coincidence of our first observations on the effects of Dee's brain damage at a time when several new developments were emerging in the neuroscience of visually guided movement, opened our eyes to the theoretical notions that were crystallized in our previous book together, *The Visual Brain in Action* (Oxford University Press, 1995). The present book is an attempt to bring those ideas, in an updated form, to a wider audience.

We continue to enjoy the unfailingly cooperative and good-humored help of Dee and Carlo. We are deeply grateful to Dee for sharing her visual world with us and for spending many long hours in the laboratory. We owe them both a deep debt of gratitude. They have taught us not only about the visual brain, but also how people can overcome the most devastating of problems with fortitude, and still enjoy a full and happy life. As with all of the brain-damaged patients we describe in the book, Dee's name is fictitious, retaining only her true initials.

We also acknowledge the help at both intellectual and practical levels of many of our colleagues, past and present, especially including (in alphabetic order): Salvatore Aglioti, David Carey, Jason Connolly, Jody Culham, Chris Dijkerman, Richard Dyde, Angela Haffenden, Monika Harvey, David Heeley, Yaoping Hu, Keith Humphrey, Lorna Jakobson, Tom James, Marc Jeannerod, Jonathan Marotta, Rob McIntosh, François Michel, Mark Mon-Williams, Kelly Murphy, David Perrett, Yves Rossetti and Philip Servos. We also owe a special thanks to Lynne Mitchell for taking care of all the details associated with arranging Dee's many visits to Canada.

We would also like to thank Jonathan Cant, Tzvi Ganel, Paul Milner, Severino Poletto, and Leon Surette for their insightful comments on earlier drafts of the manuscript—and Kenneth Valyear, Tim Andrews, Eugene McSorley and Jennifer Steeves for their assistance in preparing the figures and illustrations.

CONTENTS

Prologue

Vision, more than any other sense, dominates our mental life. Our visual experience is so rich and detailed that we can hardly distinguish that experience from the world itself. Even when we are just thinking about the world and not looking at it directly, we cannot help imagining what it *looks* like.

But where does that rich visual experience come from? Most of us have the strong impression that we are simply looking out at the world and registering what we see—as if we were nothing more than a rather sophisticated camera that delivers a faithful reproduction of the world on some kind of television screen inside our heads. This idea that we have an internal picture of the world is compelling, yet it turns out to be not only misleading but fundamentally wrong.

There is much more to vision than just pointing our eyes at the world and having the image projected onto an internal screen. Our brain has to make sense of the world, not simply reproduce it. In fact, the brain has to work just as hard to make sense of what's on a television screen in our living room as it does to make sense of the real world itself. So putting the television screen in the brain doesn't explain anything. (Who is looking at the screen in our heads?) But an even more fundamental problem is that our visual *experience* is not all there is to vision. It turns out that some of the most important things that vision does for us never reach consciousness at all.

One way to get a handle on how vision works is to study what happens when it goes wrong—not just when it goes wrong in the eye but when it goes wrong in the brain. Studying the visual life of people with certain kinds of brain damage has revealed just how misleading our intuitions about how vision works can be.

In some cases it is easy to get a feel for what such individuals might experience; in others, as is the case with the woman we are calling 'Dee Fletcher' in this book, it can be startlingly difficult to see the world through their eyes.

When we study how brain damage can disturb vision, we do not need to restrict ourselves to wondering how it affects *conscious visual experience*. Of course that is what the brain-damaged person will tell us about. When they talk about their visual problems, they are describing their conscious experience of the world—like the rest of us, they can describe only what they are aware of. But there are other ways of finding out what people can see. If we look at their behavior rather than simply listening to what they tell us, we may discover that they have other visual problems not apparent to their own awareness—or in other cases that they may be able to see far more than they think they can.

Trying to understand the visual problems that brain damage can cause leads directly to a more fundamental question: why do we need vision in the first place? In this book, we take the view that we need vision for two quite different but complementary reasons. On the one hand, we need vision to give us detailed knowledge of the world beyond ourselves—knowledge that allows us to recognize things from minute to minute and day to day. On the other hand, we also need vision to guide our actions in that world at the very moment they occur. These are two quite different job descriptions, and nature seems to have given us two different visual systems to carry them out. One system, the one that allows us to recognize objects and build up a database about the world, is the one we are more familiar with, the one that gives us our conscious visual experience. The other, much less studied and understood, provides the visual control we need in order to move about and interact with objects. This system does not have to be conscious, but it does have to be quick and accurate.

The idea of two visual systems in a single brain might initially seem counterintuitive or even absurd. It might even seem incredible to the layperson. Indeed, the idea has not even been seriously entertained as a hypothesis by most visual scientists until very recently. Our visual experience of the world is so compelling that it is hard to believe that some other quite independent visual system—one that operates completely outside of consciousness—is guiding our movements. It seems intuitively obvious that the visual image that allows us to recognize a coffee cup is the same one that guides our hand when we pick it up. But this belief is an illusion. As we will try to show in this book, the visual system that gives us our visual experience of the world is *not* the same system that guides our movements in the world.

A tragic accident

It was a bright morning in St. Andrews, Scotland, in May 1988 when we first heard about Dee Fletcher. We received an unexpected phone call from a colleague at the University of Aberdeen. He had recently returned from Milan where he had heard about a young Scottish woman who had suffered a tragic accident at her new home in Italy. Apparently, the accident had severely affected her ability to see. She had recently returned to Scotland to stay for a few months with her parents. Would we be interested in examining her? We said we would be happy to help out, although her case did not sound promising from a research point of view. Her case looked even less promising when copies of the results of clinical testing carried out in Italy arrived in the mail soon afterwards. Dee had clearly suffered a severe loss of visual function. Her visual problems were not restricted to a single domain such as the ability to recognize faces or to read words—the kind of selective loss that has long held a fascination for psychologists and other scientists interested in how the brain works. Nevertheless we fixed a date to see her.

A few days later, Dee Fletcher arrived at our St Andrews laboratory. Her mother, who understandably was extremely upset at what had happened to her only daughter, accompanied her. Dee, a small, smartly dressed woman in her early 30s, seemed a bit reserved at first, but soon began to share her unhappy story with us. Dee spoke with the assurance of a well-educated and confident individual, but one who was nevertheless clearly puzzled and distressed about her condition. As she and her mother described her life and how it had been so completely changed by a freak accident, we were able to piece together what had happened.

Dee was born and spent her early years in Scotland, but went on to spend a large part of her life in other countries—in the

Caribbean and in Africa where her father had held a number of academic posts. She now lived in Italy, where she had settled down with her partner Carlo, an Italian engineer whom she had met in Nigeria. Dee had completed a college degree in business studies, and this degree, coupled with her fluency in Italian (and several other languages) had enabled her to work as a freelance commercial translator in Italy. She had clearly been an active and lively person with many interests. While in Africa, she had become an accomplished horsewoman and, in the last two years, had learned to fly a private plane. She and her partner had enjoyed a full and happy life. Sadly, one fateful day in February 1988, their life changed forever.

On that day, Dee had been taking a shower in the newly renovated house that she and Carlo had bought in a small village north of Milan. The water for the shower was heated by a propane gas heater—a common practice in many homes in southern Europe even now. As it turned out, this particular heater was improperly vented and carbon monoxide slowly accumulated in the bathroom. Dee, of course, was unable to detect the fumes, which are quite odorless, and she eventually collapsed into a coma as the carbon monoxide displaced the oxygen in her blood. There is little doubt she would have died of asphyxiation had Carlo not arrived home just in time to save her. He gave her the kiss of life and rushed her to the local hospital, and she survived. Possibly she would have suffered less brain damage if she could have gained more specialized treatment at that early stage; but at least she survived.

The vast majority of people who survive carbon monoxide poisoning show little if any noticeable neurological effects. It was obvious to Carlo, however, as soon as Dee regained consciousness, that she was not among that fortunate majority, and he feared the worst. While she seemed alert and could speak and understand what was said to her, she could see nothing. The initial diagnosis of local doctors was therefore 'cortical blindness'. This is a condition caused by damage to the primary visual area at the back of the brain, depriving the individual of all visual experience. But gradually in the days following her arrival in the hospital, Dee began to regain some conscious sight. The first visual experience that she recalls having is a vivid sensation of color. Dee could see the red and green colors of the flowers in the vase

6

Box 1.1   Carbon monoxide poisoning

Carbon monoxide (CO) is an invisible odorless gas that is produced whenever fuels such as gasoline, oil, propane or wood
are burned. Dangerous amounts of CO can accumulate when
fuel-burning appliances are not properly vented. Carbon
monoxide poisoning occurs because CO displaces blood-borne
oxygen (by competing successfully with the oxygen molecule
for sites on the hemoglobin molecule). The most common
symptoms of CO poisoning are headache, dizziness, weakness,
nausea, vomiting, chest pain and confusion. High levels of
carbon monoxide can cause loss of consciousness and death. In
fact, CO poisoning is the number one cause of unintentional
poisoning deaths in the world. The main way CO kills is by
depriving the brain of oxygen. In other words, CO poisoning
causes anoxia.

Anoxia is a condition in which there is an absence of oxygen
supply to an organ's tissues even though there is adequate
blood flow to the organ. Hypoxia is a milder form of anoxia.
The brain is particularly sensitive to the loss of oxygen and
brain cells cannot function without oxygen for more than a
few minutes.

beside her bed and the blue and white of the sky outside.
She remarked to Carlo that he was wearing the same blue sweater
he had worn the day before. Clearly, Dee did not have cortical
blindness.

Nevertheless, Mrs Fletcher, who had flown out to Italy to be
with her daughter, was devastated when she walked into the
hospital room and Dee looked at her but did not recognize who
she was. Dee immediately recognized her voice, however, and
Mrs Fletcher was relieved to discover as she talked to her daughter that Dee could still remember everyday things and talk about
them in her usual way. She realized that while Dee's problems
were serious, they seemed to be largely restricted to seeing things
properly and making sense of them. For example, Dee had no
trouble telling what things were when she picked them up and
explored them by touch.

The following day, Dee and her mother talked together over coffee. As Mrs Fletcher passed a cup to her daughter, Dee said something rather startling. 'You know what's peculiar, Mum?' she said. 'I can see the tiny hairs on the back of your hand quite clearly!' This surprising remark led her mother to think that perhaps Dee's sight was on the road to a full recovery. But her pleasure was short-lived, when Dee added that despite seeing those fine details, she could not make out the shape of her mother's hand as a whole. In fact it soon became apparent that Dee was completely lost when it came to the shape and form of things around her. Unless an object had a distinctive color, or visual texture or grain, she had no idea what it was. Over the next few days and weeks it became painfully clear to all concerned that Dee's vision was no longer improving.

Vision without shape

As we heard this story, it became apparent to us that Dee's visual problems could not be due to a general deterioration in her visual system caused by diffuse brain damage that affected everything. For one thing, even though she could not use shape to tell one object from another, she could still use their surface detail and color. This ability to see surface properties was confirmed in formal testing that we later carried out on Dee in St Andrews. We found that she could not only name colors correctly but was also able to make fine discriminations between different shades of the same color. She could also distinguish the surface features of many objects, allowing her to identify the material they were made from (see Plate 1, top). So she might say that an object was made of red plastic or out of shiny metal—but at the same time she could only guess at its shape or function. In some cases, however, color and surface features can be highly diagnostic of what kind of object a picture represents (like the yellow color of a banana or the tiny seeds on the surface of a strawberry; see Plate 1 (bottom) for another example).

We tested Dee's ability to see fine detail (like the hairs on her mother's hand and the tiny seeds on the strawberry) by showing her patterns of lines on a computer screen (see Figure 1.1). She did as well as a visually normal person in detecting a circular patch of closely spaced fine lines on a background that had the same average brightness. Yet, remarkably, even though she could see that there was a patch of lines there, Dee was completely

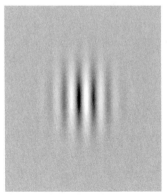

Figure 1.1

Examples of the several 'grating' patterns used to test Dee's vision for fine detail. The number of stripes per unit distance is called the spatial frequency of the pattern—the grating on the left has a low spatial frequency, the one on the right has a high spatial frequency. For each pattern, we determined the degree of contrast between dark and light stripes that was needed for Dee to see it reliably against a gray background with the same overall brightness. Dee did remarkably well in detecting these faint patterns, especially at the high spatial frequencies, but she could not reliably tell us whether the stripes were horizontal, vertical, or oblique.

unable to say whether the lines were horizontal or vertical. The fact that she could see detail just as well as a person with normal sight ruled out one obvious explanation of the problem she had in recognizing the shapes of objects. It could not be the case that her vision was simply a blur—as it would be for a short-sighted person without their eye glasses. Dee, unlike the person with myopia, could see the detail. It was the edges and outlines of objects that she couldn't make out. Her difficulty in telling even horizontal from vertical lines shows just how extreme this deficit was.

Dee has never regained a full and integrated experience of the visual world. The world she sees still lacks shape and form. So even today, more than fifteen years after the accident, Dee is unable to identify objects on the basis of their form alone. She has never, for example, been able to recognize short printed words on paper, or the faces of her friends and relatives, nor drawings or photographs of everyday objects. She has enormous difficulty in following a program on television, especially one in black and white, though she enjoys listening to audio cassettes of novels, read by an actor or the author, intended for the visually impaired.

We discovered that Dee even had problems in separating an object from its background—a basic first step for the brain in working out what an object is. Dee said that objects seemed to 'run into each other', so that two adjacent objects of a similar color such as a knife and fork will often look to her like a single indefinable 'blob'. Conversely, she will sometimes see two differently colored parts of a single object as two different objects.

Early on, we found that Dee had difficulty naming even the simplest geometrical shapes, like a triangle, a square, an oblong or a diamond. We began by showing her line drawings of shapes, or filled-in black shapes on a white background. But she was no better when we showed her shapes that differed from their backgrounds in color instead of brightness. In other words, although she could see the colors all right, she couldn't make out the edges between them. Neither could she recognize a shape made up of random dots where the dots making up the shape were textured differently from the background. Nor could she see 'shape from motion' where a patch of dots is moved against a background of stationary dots. A person with normal vision will see the shape immediately, even though it rapidly 'disappears' once the motion has stopped. Dee too saw something moving under these circumstances, and could tell us in which direction—but was quite unable to tell us what the shape was. To cut a long story short, it did not matter how a shape was defined, whether by brightness, color, texture or motion, Dee still could not recognize it (see Plate 1, middle).

Dee's difficulty in identifying objects or line drawings is not one of finding the right name for the object, nor is it one of knowing or remembering what common objects look like. Her problem is more fundamentally 'visual' than that. Dee has enormous difficulties in copying drawings of common objects or geometric shapes (see Figure 1.2). Some patients who are unable to identify pictures of objects can still slavishly copy what they see, line by line, and produce a recognizable product. But Dee cannot even pick out the constituent elements of a picture in order to copy them. Presumably unlike those patients, then, Dee's problem is not one of *interpreting* a clear visual experience—her problem is that she doesn't have that clear visual experience to start with.

Also, despite her copying problems, Dee can draw pictures of many common objects from memory. For example, when asked to 'draw an apple' or 'draw a house', she does this quite well. Her drawings are by no means perfect, but then it is almost as if she is drawing with her eyes closed, because she does not appreciate visually what she is drawing. It is not surprising that sometimes

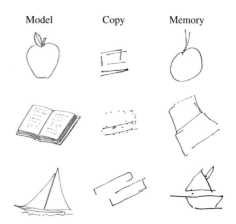

Figure 1.2

Dee was able to recognize none of the three drawings on the left. In fact as the middle column shows, she could not even make recognizable copies of the drawings. When she tried to copy the book Dee did incorporate some of the elements from the original drawing—the small dots representing text, for example—but her copy as a whole was poorly organized. After all, she had no idea what she was copying. Dee's inability to copy the drawings was not due to a failure to control her finger and hand movements as she moved the pencil on the paper, since on another occasion, when asked to draw (for example) an apple from memory, she produced reasonable renditions, as shown in the right-hand column. Dee was presumably able to do this because she still has memories of what objects like apples look like. Yet when she was later shown her own drawings from memory, she had no idea what they were. From Milner, A.D. & Goodale, M.A. (1995). Visual Brain in Action, Oxford University Press (Figure 5.2).

the parts of the drawing are misaligned, because when she lifts the pencil from the page she does not always put it back again in the right place. But the fact that she does as well as she does must mean that her problem with copying drawings is not that she has lost her ability to draw, nor is it that she has lost her general knowledge of what objects look like. Needless to say, when she is shown drawings that she has produced herself she is no better at recognizing these than any other drawings.

When Dee is 'drawing from memory' she can rely on visual experiences she had before her accident. It seems that Dee has as rich a store of visual memories and visual knowledge as anyone else—apart from the fact that these memories have not been updated with new visual information during the years since her accident. (Of course she would also still be constantly reminded of the shapes of small everyday objects through her sense of touch from handling them now and then.) This general knowledge about the appearance of objects enables her to bring visual images of familiar things into consciousness and talk and think about them.

The ability to see things 'in our mind's eye' allows us to carry out mental operations on objects when the objects are not actually present. Suppose you are asked to say whether a particular animal has a tail that is longer than its body. You will probably do this by conjuring up a visual image of the animal. Examining this image allows you to say that a mouse, for example, has a tail longer than its body, while a cow does not. Dee can do this just as well as most people, and unfailingly comes up with the right answers. She can even do things involving more complex mental operations. Take the following case: 'Think of the capital letter D; now imagine that it has been rotated flat-side down; now put it on top of the capital letter V; what does it look like?' Most people will say 'an ice-cream cone'—and so does Dee.

So Dee can imagine things that her brain damage prevents her from seeing. This must mean that manipulating images in the mind's eye does not depend on exactly the same parts of the brain that allow us to see things out there in the world. After all, if visual imagination did depend on those brain structures, then Dee should not have been able to imagine things at all—at least visually.

Not only can Dee deliberately form mental images, but she also finds herself doing so involuntarily at night when dreaming. She often reports experiencing a full visual world in her dreams, as rich in people, objects, and scenes as her dreams used to be before the accident. Waking up from dreams like this, especially in the early years, was a depressing experience for her. Remembering her dream as she gazed around the bedroom, she was cruelly reminded of the visual world she had lost.

Visual agnosia

Dee's basic problem is in recognizing shapes. In cases such as hers, where brain damage causes a disturbance in people's ability to recognize things, the disorder is known as 'agnosia'. This term was coined in the late nineteenth century by a then little-known neurologist named Sigmund Freud. He borrowed two elements from the ancient Greek (*a* = not, and *gnosis* = knowledge), in order to convey the idea that patients of this kind have a problem in making sense of what they see. Although we are focusing here on visual deficits, agnosias can be found in other senses, such as touch and hearing. Within vision itself, agnosia can be limited to particular visual categories, such as faces, places, or even words.

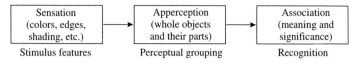

Sensation (colors, edges, shading, etc.)	Apperception (whole objects and their parts)	Association (meaning and significance)
Stimulus features	Perceptual grouping	Recognition

Figure 1.3

During the nineteenth century, the prevailing view was that we put together our raw sensations into percepts, and then attach associations to these to give them significance. Heinrich Lissauer believed that either of these two links could be severed to cause a brain-damaged person to lose the ability to recognize what he or she saw. If the first link was broken, then the person would have 'apperceptive agnosia', while if the second was broken he or she would have 'associative agnosia'. We retain broadly the same ideas today, though the terminology is different.

Even before Freud wrote about it, a distinction had been made by the German neurologist Heinrich Lissauer between two forms of agnosia (which at that time was called 'mind-blindness' or *Seelenblindheit*). According to Lissauer, agnosia could be caused by a disconnection either between perception and meaning, on the one hand, or between sensation and perception on the other (see Figure 1.3). The influential MIT neuroscientist Hans-Lukas Teuber characterized the first of these disorders (what is generally called 'associative' agnosia) as one that left people with 'percepts stripped of their meaning'. In other words, although their visual experience was intact, patients with associative agnosia could no longer attach meaning to that experience. To imagine what this would be like, think about what a typical Westerner experiences when faced with a Chinese ideogram. This symbol—full of meaning for a Chinese speaker—would be perfectly well perceived, but nonetheless remain a meaningless and puzzling pattern for the Westerner. A patient with associative agnosia would presumably react the same way when faced with a drawing of a common object such as a telephone or a bicycle. They would be able to copy the picture quite accurately (as we could do with an ideogram), but they would not have the slightest inkling of what it was they were drawing.

The other kind of agnosia that Lissauer described, which he conceptualized as a disconnection between sensation and perception, is generally called 'apperceptive' agnosia. In making this distinction between sensation and perception, Lissauer was using psychological concepts that were fashionable at the time. For the nineteenth-century thinker, sensation meant the raw sensory qualities like the color, motion, and brightness of objects or their parts, while perception referred to the process that put all of these elements together to create our visual experience, or 'percept', of an object, such as a table or a tree. A patient with apperceptive agnosia, then, would not perceive the world properly, though he or she might have perfectly intact sensory data. Because their brain cannot reconstruct the world from the information their eyes provide, they would be unable to copy line drawings of tables, trees, or even simple geometric shapes.

Nowadays Lissauer's rationale for the distinctions he was making is regarded as a little simplistic. He perhaps put too much emphasis on what today would be called 'bottom-up' processing, in which the percept is constructed directly from an analysis of the pattern of light falling on the eye. Today most visual scientists believe that such bottom-up processing, while certainly necessary, is far from sufficient for perception. They argue that what we see is also shaped by what we know about the world: in other words that learning, memory, and expectations play a crucial role in molding our perceptions. The contribution of these influences from the brain's knowledge-base about the world is often referred to as 'top-down' processing. The final percept is a combination of both current sensory input and stored information from past experience (see Plate 2, top).

Despite these reservations, most clinicians would agree that Lissauer's classification scheme still provides a useful rule of thumb for distinguishing between different levels of agnosia. Dee, of course, would fall into Lissauer's 'apperceptive' category. Her percepts are certainly not normal, and she certainly cannot produce recognizable copies of line drawings. So Dee's problems correspond well with Lissauer's conception of apperceptive agnosia. But since Lissauer's time, the designation 'apperceptive agnosia' has been used by different writers to refer to a range of different perceptual problems, not all of which involve such a basic disorder of shape perception. To avoid confusion, therefore, we will avoid using the phrase altogether. Instead, we will follow the neurologists Frank Benson and J. P. Greenberg of Boston University, who in 1969 coined the more suitably descriptive term 'visual form agnosia' for a famous patient of theirs whose basic problem, like Dee's, lay in perceiving visual form or shape. In fact, their patient, who was systematically studied by the American psychologist Robert Efron in a seminal paper also published in 1969, was uncannily similar to Dee Fletcher in a

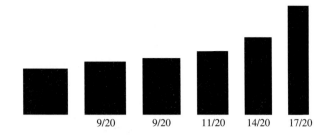

9/20   9/20   11/20   14/20   17/20

Figure 1.4

Efron's rectangles: these all have the same surface area but differ in shape. Dee was tested with several different rectangles, each in a separate test run. On each trial, she was shown a pair of shapes, either two squares, two rectangles, or one of each (with the square either on the right or the left). She was asked to say whether the two shapes were the same or different. When we used either of the two rectangles that were most similar to the square, she performed at chance level. She sometimes even made mistakes when we used the most elongated rectangle, despite taking a long time to decide. Under each rectangle is the number of correct judgments (out of 20) that Dee made in a test run with that particular rectangle.

number of ways. 'Mr. S' (as Efron referred to him) had suffered a carbon-monoxide poisoning accident while taking a shower, just like Dee did 25 years later. And like Dee, he was able to distinguish colors, but was quite unable to distinguish among geometric shapes.

Efron devised what is now a standard diagnostic test of visual form agnosia (see Figure 1.4). He wanted to measure the degree of disability a patient had in distinguishing shapes, and this meant he needed a test whose level of difficulty could be scaled, so that he could compare the degree of deficit in different patients. He hit upon the idea of creating a series of rectangular shapes that varied in length and width but not in area. These objects could be distinguished only by attending to their relative dimensions, not to their overall size. We have tested Dee using these shapes on a number of different occasions over the years. She still has great difficulty in telling pairs of these 'Efron' shapes apart, and even when she gets them right, she seems to arrive at her decision through a long and arduous process far removed from the immediacy of normal visual perception.

Summary

After three sessions of testing in our St Andrews laboratory, it was obvious to us that Dee had a profound visual form agnosia. At the same time, her memory, her ability to express herself verbally and her senses of hearing and touch were all remarkably unaffected by the asphyxia that had devastated her visual experience of the world. And even here the damage was selective, with only some aspects of visual experience being affected. Her experience of color and the surface 'texture' of objects seemed to be relatively normal. In other words, Dee's visual form agnosia appeared to be an unusually pure one. It was also obvious to us from the moment she walked into our laboratory that Dee did not suffer from any serious motor disability. That is, she had no problems walking or using her hands to pick things up. In fact, all her motor abilities seemed normal—which is often not the case in other patients who have survived near-asphyxiation. As we shall see in the next chapter, this sparing of Dee's motor system turned out to be highly significant for our further investigations.

Doing without seeing

The picture painted in Chapter 1 is a gloomy one. Dee's brain damage left her with a profoundly diminished visual life. Not only is she unable to recognize her friends and relatives, she cannot even tell the difference between simple shapes like squares and rectangles or triangles and circles. Indeed, a task as straightforward as distinguishing between horizontal and vertical lines defeats her completely. Given such a profound disability, the prognosis when we first met Dee was discouraging. Most clinicians would have classified her as legally blind, relegating her to a life in which she would need a white cane—or even a guide dog—in order to move about. After all, she could not identify anything on the basis of its shape or form. How could she possibly be expected to use her eyes to do even simple everyday tasks, such as eating a meal? Of course, many blind people can manage such tasks quite well by non-visual means. But would she, like a blind person, have to rely entirely on memory and the sense of touch?

This scenario, happily enough, has not materialized. Quite remarkably, Dee behaves in many everyday situations as though she sees perfectly well. We caught our first glimpse of Dee's preserved visual skills during one of the early testing sessions in St Andrews, back in the summer of 1988. At that time, we were showing her various everyday objects to see whether she could recognize them, without allowing her to feel what they were. When we held up a pencil, we were not surprised that she couldn't tell us what it was, even though she could tell us it was yellow. In fact, she had no idea whether we were holding it horizontally or vertically. But then something quite extraordinary happened. Before we knew it, Dee had reached out and taken the pencil, presumably to examine it more closely (see Figure 2.1). After a few moments, it dawned on us what an amazing event we had just

Figure 2.1

The examiner (on the right) held a pencil either vertically (top picture) or horizontally (bottom). Even though Dee could only guess whether the pencil was vertical or horizontal, she always grasped it perfectly.

witnessed. By performing this simple everyday act she had revealed a side to her vision which, until that moment, we had never suspected was there. Dee's movements had been quick and perfectly coordinated, showing none of the clumsiness or fumbling that one might have expected in someone whose vision was as poor as hers. To have grasped the pencil in this skillful way, she must have turned her wrist 'in flight' so that her fingers and thumb were well positioned in readiness for grasping the pencil—just like a fully sighted person. Yet it was no fluke: when we took the pencil back and asked her to do it again, she always grabbed it perfectly, no matter whether we held the pencil horizontally, vertically, or obliquely.

Dee's ability to perform this simple act presented a real paradox. How could she see the location, orientation, and shape of the pencil well enough to posture her hand correctly as she reached out to grasp it, while at the same time she couldn't tell us what she saw? She certainly could not have grasped the pencil accurately *without* using vision. A blind person couldn't have done it, nor could a sighted person wearing a blindfold. For her to have grasped the pencil so deftly, her brain must have had all kinds of advance information about where it was and what it looked like. Since there was no other way she could know how we were holding the pencil, Dee had to be using vision. Yet at the same time it was clear that she wasn't using *conscious* vision. It was this serendipitous observation that first made us suspect that Dee had visual abilities that even she was not aware of—abilities that had survived her loss of conscious visual experience.

Once we had realized what had happened, we began to notice new examples of Dee's amazing visual abilities every time we met with her. The contrast between what she could *perceive* and what she could actually *do* with her sense of vision could not have struck us more forcibly than it did one day when a group of us went out on a picnic while visiting her in Italy. We had spent the morning at her home carrying out a series of visual tests, recording one failure after another. Dee was unable to recognize any of the faces, patterns, or drawings we showed to her. Again it was obvious that the only way Dee could even tell one person from another was by looking at the color of their hair or their clothing. It had been a frustrating morning for her.

To lighten the gloom, Carlo suggested that we all go for a picnic in the Italian Alps, to a popular spot not far from their home.

We drove high up into the mountains, until the massive peak of Monrosa loomed into view. We parked the car and then set off on foot to reach our picnic site—an alpine meadow higher up on the side of the mountain. This walk provided a good example of a time when the other side of Dee's visual life was strikingly revealed. To reach the meadow, we had to walk along a half-mile trail through a dense pine forest. The footpath was steep and uneven. Yet Dee had no trouble at all. She walked confidently and unhesitatingly, without stumbling, tripping over a root, or colliding with the branches of the trees that hung over the path. Occasionally we had to point out to her the correct route to take, but other than that, her behavior was indistinguishable from that of any of the other hikers on the mountain that day.

We eventually arrived at the meadow and began to unpack the picnic hamper. Here Dee displayed once more how apparently normal her visual behavior was. She reached out to take things that were passed to her with the same confidence and skill as someone with completely normal sight. No-one would ever have guessed that she could not see the difference between a knife and a fork, or recognize the faces of her companions.

The mailbox

Needless to say, scientific colleagues are seldom convinced by anecdotes like these, however compelling they might seem at the time. We had to demonstrate Dee's visual skills in the laboratory. We had to show that even though she was unable to recognize objects or even tell them apart, this did not prevent her from using vision to guide her actions directed at those objects. And this meant introducing both objective measurement and experimental control. Our first attempt to do this was inspired by that remarkable day when she reached out and grasped a pencil during our preliminary tests of object recognition. Refining a test first described by Marie-Thérèse Perenin and Alain Vighetto (see Chapter 3), we set up a simple piece of apparatus where we could ask Dee to 'post' a card into an open slot—like a mailbox, but with the added feature that the slot could be presented at different orientations, not just at the horizontal (see Figure 2.2). On each occasion, she had no way of knowing ahead of time what the orientation of the slot would be when she opened her eyes to look at it.

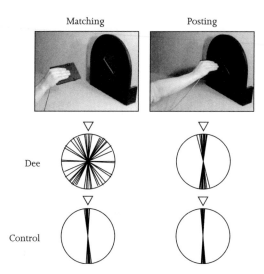

Figure 2.2

Matching and posting tasks. Dee was presented with a vertical display with a slot cut into it which could be rotated to different orientations. In the 'matching' task, she was asked to turn a hand-held card so that it matched with the orientation of the slot, without reaching out toward the display. In the 'posting' task, she was asked to reach out and 'post' the card into the slot. As shown in the diagrams below the pictures, Dee had no problem with the posting task, but performed almost randomly on the matching task. Healthy control subjects, of course, had no problem with either task. (Although the slot was presented in several different orientations, the diagrams always show 'correct' as vertical.) From Goodale, M.A., Milner, A.D., Jakobson, L.S., & Carey, D.P. (1991). A neurological dissociation between perceiving objects and grasping them. *Nature*, 349, 154–156 (Figure 1).

When tested in this way, Dee performed remarkably well, whatever the orientation of the slot. Indeed the accuracy of her behavior was almost indistinguishable from that of several people with unimpaired vision that we tested. Dee moved her hand forward unhesitatingly, and almost always inserted the card smoothly into the slot. Moreover, video recordings revealed that she began to rotate the card toward the correct orientation well in advance of arriving at the slot. In other words, she was using vision right from the start to guide her movements—just as anyone with normal vision would do. Over the years, we have tested her on several versions of this test and her behavior always looks normal, however we measure it.

Given what we knew about Dee's visual abilities, we were pretty sure that she wouldn't be able to tell us about the different orientations of the slot—even though she was inserting the card into it so accurately. But we had to check this formally. In our first attempt to do this, we simply asked her to tell us what the orientation of the slot was—was it horizontal, vertical, or tilted to the left or right? Most of the time she appeared to have little idea of the slot's orientation and ended up simply guessing. For example, she was just as likely to say that a vertical slot was horizontal as she was to get it right. But this was still not convincing enough— maybe her problem was not so much a visual one but rather one of putting what she saw into words. So in another test, we asked her to tell us the orientation by simply lifting the card up and turning it to match the orientation of the slot, but without making a reaching movement toward the slot. Here we were not asking her to use words to *tell* us what she saw, but to use a hand movement to *show* us what she saw. But the videotapes we made of her hand movements told much the same story as her verbal descriptions. In other words, the angles at which she held the card showed no relationship at all to the actual orientation of the slot.

Her failure to 'match' the slot correctly using the card was not because she could not rotate her hand properly to indicate a particular orientation. We were able to rule out that possibility by asking her to *imagine* a slot at different orientations. Once she had done this, she had no difficulty rotating the card to show us the orientation she had been asked to imagine. It was only when she had to look at a real slot and match its orientation that her deficit appeared.

These first experimental tests confirmed our suspicions that something very interesting was going on. Dee could turn her hand correctly so that the card would pass smoothly into the slot, but she could not make a similar rotation of her hand to convey to us the orientation of the slot that she saw in front of her. But this was just the beginning of the story.

Grasping size

The posting test showed that Dee had good visual control of her hand movements when confronted with an oriented slot. Of course whenever we pick up a pencil we unthinkingly tailor the orientation of our hand to the orientation of the pencil. At the same time, we also calibrate the separation of our finger and thumb as we move our hand toward the pencil. We do all this quite automatically. In fact, our hand and fingers begin to adopt the final posture of the grasp well before we make contact. In doing this, the advance information we use has to be visual—particularly when we are confronted with the object for the first time and so we have no memory of it to fall back on.

The exquisite tuning of the hand to the target of the grasp was first documented in detail by the French neuroscientist Marc Jeannerod. He made high-speed films of normal individuals reaching out to grasp solid objects like balls and cylinders of different sizes. By then looking at individual frames of film, he was able to reconstruct the entire trajectory of the grasping movement from start to finish. These reconstructions revealed a beautifully orchestrated action. As soon as the hand left the table en route to the object, the fingers and thumb began to open (see Figure 2.3). Then, about two-thirds of the way toward the object, they began to close in on the object so that a smooth and accurate grasp was achieved. Even though the maximum opening between the fingers and thumb was much larger than the width of the object itself, Jeannerod showed that the two were closely related: the bigger the object, the bigger the maximum grip size (see Figure 2.4).

So the obvious next question to ask was this: Would Dee demonstrate the same relationship between grip size and object size that Jeannerod had demonstrated in healthy people—even though she has no conscious visual experience of the dimensions of the objects?

Figure 2.3

This sequence shows a hand reaching out to grasp a rectangular block. Notice that the finger and thumb first open wider than the block and then close down as the hand approaches the block.

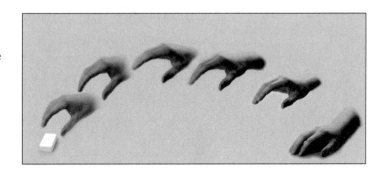

Figure 2.4

Not only do we rotate our hand in the correct orientation as we reach out to grasp an object, but the opening between our thumb and fingers is scaled to the object's size. Thus, we open our hand wider in flight to pick up a beaker than we do to pick up a measuring cylinder.

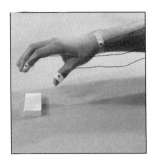

Figure 2.5

A grasping hand open to its widest extent (maximum grip aperture) as the subject reaches out to grasp one of the three-dimensional Efron blocks. Small infrared-emitting markers have been attached to the ends of the finger and thumb and to the wrist. These markers are tracked with infrared-sensitive cameras.

We had already noticed that she had no difficulty picking up everyday objects of many different shapes and sizes, from pencils to coffee cups. But to test this more formally, we had to come up with some objects where the dimensions could be varied but the overall size of the object did not change. Also, it was important to use objects that had no meaning, so that she couldn't simply remember what kind of grasp was required by guessing what the object was. For example, she might guess that she was picking up a pencil from its yellow color, or a coffee cup because she remembered putting it down on the table. The solution we came up with was to make three-dimensional versions of the rectangles devised by Robert Efron that we described in Chapter 1—a set of six rectangular wooden blocks that varied in width (but not in overall area). We already knew, of course, that Dee would have great difficulty distinguishing between these different shapes.

In order to monitor the movements of the hand and fingers as the reach and grasp unfolded, we were able to take advantage of new technology that had been developed in Canada. The technique involved attaching small infrared lights to the tips of the index finger and thumb. The three-dimensional coordinates of these lights could then be tracked with two infrared-sensitive cameras and stored in a computer as the hand moved out to pick up a target object (see Figure 2.5). Special computer software could then be used to plot how the finger postures changed as the hand moved toward its goal. These techniques were already in use in the visuomotor laboratory at the University of Western Ontario where one of us (Mel Goodale) was now working.

So in the spring of 1990, Dee and Carlo made their first trip to Canada, spending a week visiting London Ontario. We gave Dee a day or two to get over her jet lag, and then we brought her into the laboratory where we carried out our first test using the 'Efron blocks'. Small infrared lights were attached with adhesive tape to Dee's fingers, thumb, and wrist. We placed the shapes in front of her, one by one, and asked her simply to reach out and pick them up and put them down again. When we tracked how she opened her hand as she reached toward the object, we found that she showed exactly the same scaling of her grip 'mid-flight' as the normally sighted individuals we tested. In other words, the wider the block, the wider her hand opened. It was clear then that like anyone else, she was unconsciously using visual information to program her grasp, and doing so with considerable precision.

As expected, however, Dee found it difficult to distinguish between these solid rectangles when they were presented as pairs. She could not even show us how wide each block was by using her finger and thumb, which we were able to monitor using the same recording equipment we had used to track her grasping movements. For most people, of course, making such size estimates with the finger and thumb is a simple thing to do. But it was not for Dee. Her estimates were wildly inaccurate, and showed no relationship at all to the real width of the blocks. Yet she understood perfectly well what we were asking her to do—when we asked her to imagine a familiar object, like a Ping-Pong ball or a grapefruit, she had no trouble showing us how big that object was using her finger and thumb.

So we arrive at a similar conclusion as before: Dee seems to have no trouble in using visual information to program her grasping. Yet, at the same time, she does not have any conscious visual experience of the dimensions of the objects she is picking up so skillfully.

Grasping shape

Dee can deal proficiently with the size and orientation of objects when she has to use those features in simple behavioral actions. But what about their *shape*? Could she use the outline of an object, the very thing whose absence robs her visual experience of its essential structure, to guide her actions? For example, the rectangular shapes we had used earlier to probe her ability to scale her grasp varied not only in width but also in shape. In that earlier study, the blocks had always been placed in the same orientation and she had been instructed to pick them up front to back. This meant she did not have to use the shape—only the width—to pick up the blocks successfully. But what if they were placed in unpredictable orientations from one occasion to the next and she was given no instructions as to how to pick them up?

When we carried out a test like this, Dee did just as well as she had done when the blocks were always in the same orientation (see Figure 2.6). This meant she must have processed not only the dimensions of the object but also its orientation. In other words,

24

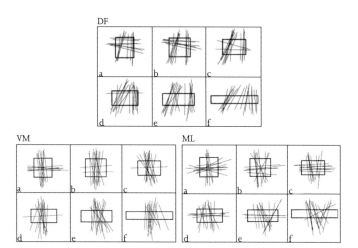

Figure 2.6

These diagrams show how Dee and two healthy control subjects picked up blocks
placed in different orientations on a table in front of them. The lines connect the
points where the index finger and thumb first made contact with the block. (The
results at the different orientations are all shown together on a standard drawing of
the block.) Just like the control subjects, when Dee reached out to pick up the block
that was nearly square, she was almost—though not quite—as likely to pick it up
lengthwise as widthwise. But with more elongated blocks, she and the control
subjects were progressively less likely to do that. None of subjects ever tried to pick
up the most elongated block lengthwise. In short, Dee was able to take both the
orientation and the shape of the block into account in planning her movement,
just like people with normal vision. From Carey, D.P., Harvey, M., & Milner (1996).
Visuomotor sensitivity for shape and orientation in a patient with visual form
agnosia. *Neuropsychologia*, 34, 329–337 (Figure 3).

she had to scale her grasp and at the same time rotate her wrist in
flight to get her finger and thumb in the right positions. We noticed
as well that she nearly always picked up the blocks widthwise
rather than lengthwise, even though we gave her no instructions to
do this. Obviously, we will pick up a square block equally often
either way, because the length is the same as the width. Less obviously, but perhaps not unreasonably, the more elongated the block,
the more we go for the width in preference to the length (other
things being equal). Dee is no exception to this. This simple fact
shows that the undamaged part of Dee's visual brain can not only
tailor her grasp to one of the dimensions of the block, but it can
work out which dimension is the shorter of the two. This computation then allows her to choose the most appropriate grasp points,
generally at right angles to the principal axis of the shape. In short,
her actions can still be guided to some degree by visual shape.

But we were interested to go further and find out whether
Dee's visuomotor system could do more than simply compute the

dimensions and orientation of regular objects. For many shapes, the visuomotor system must also take into account other geometric properties, such as the curvature of the object at different points around its edges. This is a problem that roboticists have had to address in the development of control systems for so-called 'autonomous' robots that can work in unfamiliar environments. In such situations, the robots will often be required to pick up objects that neither they nor their programmer could have anticipated. To do this the robot, like the human, has to use its optical sensors to compute not only the object's width, orientation, and principal axis but also the curvature at different places around the object's boundaries. Only by computing the convexities and concavities around the object, would the robot (or the human) be able to select the most stable grasp points—points where the robot's grippers (or the human's finger and thumb) could clasp the object securely.

Discussions with a German colleague, Heinrich Bülthoff, brought to our attention the work of Andrew Blake, an engineer at Oxford University. Blake had developed a series of abstract shapes to evaluate the performance of different computer programs he had designed to guide robotic grasping of novel objects. With Bülthoff's help we constructed what we came to refer to as the

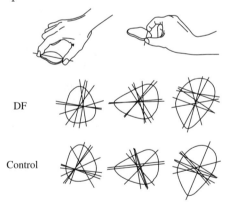

DF

Control

Figure 2.7

The Blake shapes. The drawings at the top show a stable (on the left) and an unstable (on the right) grasp for these irregular shapes. For shapes of this kind, the lines joining the index finger and thumb for a correct grasp would pass through the center of the shape and would be positioned on stable points on the edge of the shape. As the grasp lines shown on the outlines of three typical shapes illustrate, Dee grasped the shapes just as well as the control subject. From Goodale, M.A., Meenan, J.P., Bülthoff, H.H., Nicolle, D.A., Murphy, K.J., & Racicot, C.I. (1994). Separate neural pathways for the visual analysis of object shape in perception and prehension. *Current Biology*, 4(7), 604–610 (Figure 5).

'Blake shapes', a set of smooth, flat, pebble-like objects, for testing Dee's ability to select stable grasp points on unfamiliar shapes.

When we presented these shapes one by one to Dee, she had no difficulty whatever in picking them up (see Figure 2.7). As she reached to pick up each Blake shape, she made subtle adjustments in the positioning of her finger and thumb in flight so that they engaged the object at stable grasp points on its boundary. Just like people with normal vision, or one of Blake's robots, she would choose stable points the first time she was presented with each object. Yet, needless to say, she was totally at a loss when it came to saying whether pairs of these smooth objects were alike or different.

Walking around

As we saw at the beginning of this chapter, Dee is able to hike over difficult terrain as skillfully as the next person. When walking through a room, she never bumps into furniture or doorways. In fact, this apparently normal navigation through her immediate environment, coupled with her ability to reach out and shake your hand or take objects that are offered to her, makes many people who meet her for the first time doubt that she has any visual problems at all. She talks to them intelligently about her journey and she even appears to recognize people she knows in the laboratory. As a result, some colleagues who have come to test her have initially been so skeptical as to feel they were wasting their time— they could test such an apparently normal person any time!

Of course, as all psychologists should know, appearances can be deceptive. For example, Dee's recognition of people that she has met on previous occasions need not be due to any *visual* ability, but rather to her ability to remember what someone's voice sounds like. (Though it is true that she can use certain visual cues, like color. We had a colleague in St Andrews with a penchant for dyeing his hair bright colors—often more than one. Dee never had any difficulty recognizing him.) A skeptic (as psychologists are by nature) could argue likewise that in the anecdote with which we started this chapter, Dee's ability to negotiate the trail at Monrosa might owe much to her previous experience with this popular picnic spot.

So we needed a way to test her ability to walk around an unfamiliar environment, in which we could specify beforehand

Figure 2.8

A foot going over an obstacle. Note that the toe of the leading foot just clears the top of the obstacle; the same is true for the toe of the trailing foot as well. In other words, we leave just enough clearance to make sure that our foot doesn't touch the obstacle—rather than leaving a large safety margin whatever the height of the obstacle.

the precise nature of the obstacles placed in her path. Fortunately, at the University of Waterloo, only an hour away from the University of Western Ontario, a colleague of ours, Aftab Patla, was studying just this kind of locomotor skill in people with normal vision. Patla had constructed a special laboratory in which he could place obstacles of particular heights at specified points along a route that his volunteers were asked to follow. With the help of the same kind of opto-electronic equipment that we were using at Western, he was able to measure the adjustments that people automatically make to their gait as they step over such obstacles.

On one of Dee's several visits to Canada, we drove her to Waterloo where she was quite happy to try Patla's test. She walked through his test environment absolutely confidently and without tripping over any of the obstacles, which varied in height from less than an inch up to fifteen inches (see Figure 2.8). In fact her behavior was indistinguishable from that of other volunteers. Just like them, she effortlessly raised her foot just enough to clear each of the obstacles. It will come as no surprise to the reader, however, that when asked to estimate the height of the obstacles in a separate test, Dee was much less accurate than the normal volunteers.

How does she do it?

All the laboratory testing confirmed our informal observations: In one sense, Dee sees perfectly well. She uses visual information about the size, the orientation, and to some degree the shape, of objects to execute skilled movements. Yet in another sense, Dee sees nothing at all—and can certainly tell us nothing—about these attributes of the objects.

So what was the essential difference between the situations in which she succeeded and those where she failed? As pointed out earlier, it is not simply the case that she is unable to put her visual experience into words. Nor is it the case that whenever she makes some kind of skilled limb movement in response to a visible object she gets it right. Take, for example, the posting test. Her ability to insert the card into the slot cannot simply be put down to the fact that she was making a manual action. She had to make a hand movement in the matching test as well—yet she failed completely. The critical difference therefore is not that a movement was made in one case but not in the other. It is the *purpose* of the movement that matters. When we asked people to use their hand to show us what they saw in the matching test, they were reporting on their conscious perception of the slot in front of them. Turning the hand in this case was an act of communication. The fact that the communication happened to be manual was arbitrary—the same information could have been conveyed by a variety of different means. They could have drawn a line on a piece of paper, for example; or picked the correct orientation from a number of alternatives in a multiple choice test; or of course they could simply have told us in words. Dee could do none of these things—not because she couldn't communicate but because she had nothing visual to communicate. She had no conscious experience, no conscious visual experience at least, of the orientation of the slot to share with us.

The action that Dee had to make in the original posting test had a very different purpose. To get the card into the slot, she had no choice but to turn her hand in a particular direction. This rotation was an obligatory part of the action rather than being an arbitrary act of communication. Dee had to make the same kind of rotation of her wrist when she reached out to pick up a rectangular block or a pencil placed at a particular orientation. Such movements are part of an ancient repertoire that we share with our present-day primate cousins, the monkeys and apes, and presumably also with our own primate ancestors. For example, when we are standing in a crowded subway train and it suddenly jerks to a stop, we may find ourselves quickly reaching out to grasp a handrail to steady ourselves. We do this without thinking, yet our brain has to do some complex processing so that our hand can turn rapidly and accurately so as to grasp the rail. This echoes the kinds of unthinking hand movements our arboreal ancestors would have had to make when grasping branches and when foraging for food.

The most amazing thing about Dee is that she is able to use visual properties of objects such as their orientation, size and shape, to guide a range of skilled actions—despite having no conscious awareness of those same visual properties. This contrast between what she can and cannot do with visual information has important implications about how the brain deals with incoming visual signals. It indicates that some parts of the brain (which we have good reason to believe are damaged in Dee) play a critical role in giving us visual awareness of the world while other parts (relatively undamaged in her) are more concerned with the immediate visual control of skilled actions.

Perhaps this should not be too surprising. On the one hand we need vision for the on-line control of everyday actions—particularly for those actions where speed is at a premium and we do not have time to think. But on the other hand we need vision to make sense of the world around us, when we do have time to think! In fact, for most people, including most vision scientists, this perceptual experience of the world is the most important aspect of vision. What perception does for us is to translate the ever-changing array of 'pixels' on our retina into a stable world of objects that exists independent of ourselves. This allows us to construct an internal model of the external world that enables us to attach meaning and significance to objects and events, to understand their causal relations, and to remember them from day to day. Perception also allows us to plan our future actions, and to communicate with others about what we see around us.

Summary

The studies with Dee highlight the two distinct jobs that vision does for us: the control of action on the one hand, and the construction of our perceptual representations on the other. As we will see in the next two chapters, these two different functions of vision have shaped the way the visual brain has evolved. Rather than evolving some kind of general-purpose visual system that does everything, the brain has opted for two quite separate visual systems: one that guides our actions and another, quite separate system, that handles our perception.

Thinking about vision this way certainly helps us to understand Dee's predicament. The anoxic episode (see Box 1.1) profoundly affected her vision for perception but left her vision for action largely unscathed. What was lucky for us as scientists, and also of course for her, was that the damage was so specific that her vision-for-action system has continued to operate remarkably successfully in isolation. What the damage did was to uncover in Dee a system that we all use, but one that is normally overshadowed and out-shone by our concurrent visual experience of the world. Her tragic accident has allowed us to bring this visuomotor system out of the shadows, and to explore its operating characteristics and scope.

When vision for
action fails

The startling visual dissociations we have described in Dee Fletcher point to the existence of two relatively independent visual systems within the brain—one for conscious perception, which is severely damaged in Dee, and another for the unconscious control of action, which is largely preserved. But skeptics could argue that all we have documented in Dee is a case of someone with poor vision. Maybe you do not need as much visual information to guide your actions as you do to perceive and recognize people and objects. Dee's vision might be good enough for picking something up, but not good enough for telling what it is. In other words, maybe there is only one visual system, not two, and in Dee's case it is simply functioning below some threshold level. On the face of it, this might seem like a valid argument. But if it were true, then there shouldn't be any cases of brain-injured individuals who show the *opposite* pattern of deficits and spared visual abilities to that seen in Dee. It should always be conscious perception that suffers first. Yet as we shall see in this chapter, such patients do exist. Moreover, the part of the visual brain that is damaged in these individuals is quite different from that damaged in Dee.

Bálint's syndrome

Even at the beginning of the twentieth century, neurologists were describing cases of patients whose 'visual' problems could be characterized as *visuomotor* in nature. In other words, they were describing cases where a patient had a specific problem in translating vision into action. Later work has gone on to show that

Figure 3.1

The human brain showing the lateral, medial, and ventral surfaces.
Key: A anterior; P posterior;
1 Frontal lobe; 2 Parietal lobe;
3 Temporal lobe; 4 Occipital lobe;
5 Cerebellum; 6 Thalamus;
7 Superior colliculus; 8 Pons;
9 Medulla; 10 Optic nerve;
11 Corpus callosum.

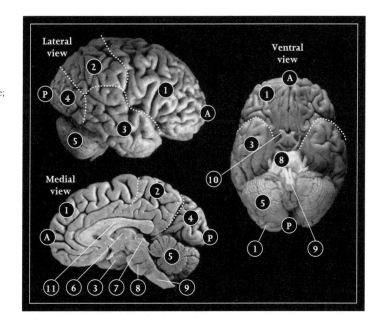

at least some of these patients show remarkably intact visual perception—despite having profound difficulties performing even simple visually guided movements. In short, the clinical picture they present is the mirror image of Dee Fletcher's.

The Hungarian neurologist Rudolph Bálint was the first to document a patient with this kind of problem, in 1909. The patient was a middle-aged man who suffered a massive stroke to both sides of the brain in a region called the parietal lobe (see Figure 3.1). Although the man complained of problems with his eyesight, he certainly was not agnosic in the way that Lissauer's and Freud's patients were. He could recognize objects and people, and could even read. He did tend to ignore objects on his left side and had some difficulty moving his eyes from one object to another. But his big problem was not a failure to recognize objects, but rather an inability to reach out and pick them up. Instead of reaching directly toward an object, he would grope in its general direction much like a blind man, often missing it by a few inches. Unlike a blind man, however, he could see the object perfectly well; he just couldn't guide his hand toward it. Bálint coined the term 'optic ataxia' (*optische Ataxie*) to refer to this problem in visually guided reaching.

Bálint's first thought was that this difficulty in reaching toward objects might be due to a general failure to locate where the objects were in his field of vision. But it turned out that the patient showed the problem only when he used his right hand. When he used his left hand to reach for the same object, his reaches were pretty accurate. This means that there could not have been a general problem in *seeing* where something was. In other words, this was not a visuospatial deficit. After further testing, Bálint discovered that the man's reaching difficulty was not a purely motor problem either—some kind of general difficulty in moving his right arm correctly. He deduced this from asking the patient to point to different parts of his own body using his right hand with his eyes closed: there was no problem.

So the optic ataxia that Bálint's patient suffered from was a truly 'visuomotor' disorder, in the sense that the patient could not use visual information about the location of the target to control a reaching movement with his (right) arm. Thus, although his deficit affected behavior directed at visual targets, it could not be explained away either as a general problem in either visuospatial processing or motor control. Unfortunately, this simple point has been largely overlooked by subsequent generations of neurologists, particularly in the English-speaking world. This may have been partly because Bálint's report remained untranslated for many years. Instead, most British and North American neurologists have followed the influential English physician and scientist, Gordon Holmes, and attributed these kinds of reaching difficulties to a general disorder in visuospatial perception—a deficit which would necessarily affect all spatially directed behavior, whatever form that behavior might take.

What has gone wrong in optic ataxia?

It was not in fact until the 1980s that the true nature of optic ataxia became apparent, in large part through the work of the French neurologists Marie-Thérèse Perenin and Alain Vighetto. They made detailed video recordings of patients with optic ataxia in a number of different visuomotor tests. Like Bálint, they observed that the patients made errors in reaching toward target objects placed in different spatial locations. Nevertheless, the patients were able to give accurate verbal descriptions of the relative location of the very objects to which they could not direct their hand. Like Bálint, Perenin and Vighetto demonstrated that

Figure 3.2

Marie-Thérèse Perenin and Alain Vighetto discovered that patients with 'optic ataxia' not only have problems reaching to point to something accurately, but also tend to direct their hand at the wrong angle when trying to pass it through a slot. The same patients, however, often have no problem describing the orientation of the slot in words.

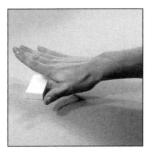

Figure 3.3

A typical example of a poor grip in a patient with optic ataxia. Her posture resembles someone groping in the dark for an object they know is there, although in this case the patient can see the object perfectly well.

the patients also had no difficulty in directing hand movements towards different parts of their body.

In another test, Perenin and Vighetto examined the ability of these patients to reach out and pass their hand through an open slot cut in a disk, which could be positioned at different orientations at random (see Figure 3.2). Not only did the patients tend to make spatial errors, in which their hand missed the slot altogether, but they also made orientation errors, in which the hand would approach the slot at the wrong angle. Yet several of these same patients could easily tell one orientation of the slot from another when asked to do so. So their failure to deal with the orientation of the slot when reaching was not due a perceptual difficulty in telling apart the different orientations. Again their problem was visuomotor in nature—in this case a problem in guiding their hand as they tried to pass it at the correct angle through the slot. (Of course when their hand made contact with the disk they could correct themselves using touch, and then pass their hand through the slot.)

As described in the previous chapter, of course, it was by borrowing Perenin and Vighetto's slot task that we were first able to provide a convincing demonstration of Dee Fletcher's preserved visuomotor abilities in the context of her profound visual form agnosia. In other words, the work with optic ataxic patients nicely complements Dee's pattern of performance on the slot task. So, does this neat contrast between the two kinds of patients also extend to the other tests we found Dee to be good at, such as grasping objects of different sizes?

Again the relevant evidence was gathered in France, in this case by Marc Jeannerod, who, as we noted in the previous chapter, pioneered the application of quantitative methods to the analysis of visually guided grasping in healthy volunteers. Importantly, Jeannerod went on to show that the well-regulated patterns of movement that typify the normal person's reaching and grasping behavior were severely disrupted in patients with optic ataxia. Instead of first opening the hand during the early part of the reach, and then gradually closing it as it moved toward the target object, the optic ataxic patient would keep the hand widely opened throughout the movement, much as a person would do if reaching blindfolded toward the object (see Figure 3.3). Just a few years ago, Jeannerod and his colleagues tested a patient,

Anne Thiérry, who has a large area of damage to the parietal lobe on both sides of the brain, very much like Bálint's original case. They used similar matching and grasping tasks to those we had used earlier with Dee. Anne was found to show poor scaling of her grip while reaching for objects of different sizes, while remaining well able to demonstrate the sizes of the objects by use of her forefinger and thumb. This result again complements perfectly our findings with Dee.

The work we have summarized so far shows that optic ataxic patients not only have problems directing their actions to visual targets in space, but also have trouble with other visuomotor tasks in which object size and orientation are the critical factors. At the same time, when asked to *distinguish between* objects on the basis of their size, orientation or relative location, many of these patients do quite well. As we saw, this pattern of behavior is the converse of what we found with Dee. And it does not end there. We tested an optic ataxic patient called Ruth Vickers with the 'Blake' shapes described in the last chapter. We were interested to see if she would show the opposite pattern of results to that shown by Dee.

Ruth was a middle-aged housewife from rural Ontario who had recently suffered two strokes, one on each side of the brain, the second stroke occurring within a week of the first. Brain imaging showed that the damage was almost symmetrically located in the parietal lobe, again rather like Bálint's patient (see Figure 3.4).

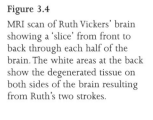

Figure 3.4

MRI scan of Ruth Vickers' brain showing a 'slice' from front to back through each half of the brain. The white areas at the back show the degenerated tissue on both sides of the brain resulting from Ruth's two strokes.

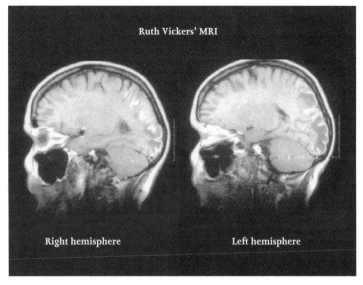

Ruth Vickers' MRI

Right hemisphere   Left hemisphere

Model   Copy

Figure 3.5

Unlike Dee, Ruth Vickers had no difficulty recognizing and naming the drawings shown on the left. Even when she was asked to copy them, she was able to capture many of the features of the drawings. Nonetheless it is obvious that she had difficulties coordinating her movements as she did her drawings.

Figure 3.6

Examples of Ruth's attempts to pick up Blake shapes. Unlike Dee, she often grasped the shapes at inappropriate points, so that the shape would slip out of her fingers. From Goodale, M.A., Meenan, J.P., Bülthoff, H.H., Nicolle, D.A., Murphy, K.J., & Racicot, C.I. (1994). Separate neural pathways for the visual analysis of object shape in perception and prehension. *Current Biology*, 4(7), 604–610 (Figure 5).

Her clinical picture initially looked very much like that described by Bálint. Although Ruth's symptoms had cleared to some degree by the time we saw her, it was obvious that she still had severe optic ataxia. She could not reach with any degree of accuracy to objects that she could see but was not looking at directly. She could, however, reach reasonably accurately to objects directly in her line of sight.

Nevertheless, the reaches Ruth made to pick up objects that she was looking at, although spatially accurate, were far from normal. Like Anne Thiérry, she would open her hand wide as she reached out, no matter how big or small the objects were, showing none of the grip scaling typically seen in normal people. Yet despite this, when asked to show us how big she thought the object was using her finger and thumb, she performed quite creditably, again just like Anne. And she could describe most of the objects and pictures we showed her without any difficulty. In fact, although her strokes had left her unable to control a pencil or pen very well, she could draw quite recognizable copies of pictures she was shown (see Figure 3.5). In other words, Ruth's visual experience of the world seemed pretty intact, and she could readily convey to us what she saw—in complete contrast to Dee Fletcher.

Because Ruth could distinguish between many different shapes and patterns, we did not expect her to have much difficulty with the smooth pebble-like shapes we had tested Dee with earlier. We were right—when she was presented with a pair of these Blake shapes she could generally tell us whether or not the two shapes were the same. Although she sometimes made mistakes, particularly when two identical shapes were presented in different orientations, her performance was much better than Dee's. When it came to picking up the shapes, however, the opposite was the case. Ruth had real problems. Instead of gripping the Blake shapes at stable 'grasp points', she positioned her finger and thumb almost at random (see Figure 3.6). This inevitably meant that after her fingers contacted the pebble she had to correct her grip by means of touch—if she did not, the pebble would often slip from her grasp. In other words, although some part of her brain could clearly analyze the shape of these objects, her hand was unable to use that information.

All of these studies help us to define what it is that has gone wrong in optic ataxia. The patients tested by Perenin, Vighetto and

Jeannerod, as well as by us, were all typical cases of this condition. Their brain damage was in the same region of the parietal lobe as that damaged in Bálint's patient, and they showed a similar inaccuracy when reaching out to targets in different parts of visual space. The fact that Perenin and Vighetto's patients could describe the location of the objects to which they could not reach supports Bálint's belief that optic ataxia was a visuomotor deficit and not, as Gordon Holmes maintained, part of larger overarching deficit in spatial perception.

But there is another important reason to doubt Holmes's account. As we have seen, many patients with optic ataxia demonstrate deficits that cannot be usefully construed as 'spatial', in the sense of seeing *where* an object is. For example, they do not rotate their wrist or open their grasp appropriately when picking up objects. Ruth Vickers, the patient we studied in Canada, could not direct her grasp to the appropriate points on the edges of the object that she was trying to pick up. In short, the range of visual attributes that are no longer accessible to the mechanisms controlling skilled motor output is much broader than originally thought, even by Bálint. So it is not useful to think about optic ataxia in terms of a deficit in spatial coding, some kind of a problem in seeing the spatial location of objects in the world. It now makes much more sense to think of it as a *visuomotor* disorder instead. To borrow some terminology from robotic engineering, optic ataxia can be seen as a disruption of the control systems connecting the sensors (dealing with the input) and the actuators (providing the output). These control systems would take all the relevant optical information from the sensors and re-code it for the programming and control of the goal-directed movements of the robot. In the human brain, analogous systems have to transform visual information about the size, shape, orientation, motion, and spatial location of the goal object, into a code for programming and controlling the person's skilled motor acts.

Summary

We have seen in this chapter that, in many different respects, optic ataxic patients present a quite opposite pattern of visual disabilities (and spared visual abilities) to what we saw in Dee Fletcher. This has important theoretical implications for our interpretation of what is going on in Dee (and indeed in the optic ataxic patients). Going back to the concern with which we began this chapter, it cannot simply be the case that brain damage degrades the quality of Dee's visual experience in an undifferentiated way, so that some tasks can still be done while other 'more difficult' ones cannot. If this were true, then Ruth and Anne should show the same pattern of deficits and spared abilities as Dee. But of course they show the opposite. There is no way that a unitary general-purpose visual system can explain this.

Conversely, the fact that Dee Fletcher shows intact visuomotor control in the face of a profound perceptual loss also undercuts a common account of what causes optic ataxia. Some scientists have argued that optic ataxia is simply a 'disconnection' between visual perception and action, in which the perceptual information just cannot get through to the motor system. According to this intuitively reasonable view, there is only one kind of visual processing, which not only provides our conscious perception, but also the visual guidance for all our actions. But if this were the case, then how could Dee, whose visual perception of object form has been lost, carry out actions based on object form? If she does not have the perception, she should not be able to perform the visually guided actions. In short, Dee's spared abilities disprove this disconnection account of optic ataxia.

The existence of opposite patterns of lost and spared abilities in two kinds of patients is known in the trade as a 'double dissociation'. What a double dissociation shows is that when brain damage impairs one task (a recognition test, for example) but not another (such as a test of visuomotor skill), that difference cannot simply be put down to the second task being easier than the first. The other half of the double dissociation (in this case a visuomotor impairment coexisting with intact visual perception) rules that out.

What a double dissociation can also suggest—but cannot prove—is that different, quasi-independent brain systems (or brain 'modules' as they are sometimes called) are handling each of the two abilities that are dissociated. Establishing such modularity requires independent evidence from other kinds of research such as brain anatomy. In the next chapter we will discuss some of the kinds of evidence that support the idea of modularity in the organization of the visual system.

The origins of vision: from modules to models

For most of us, sight is our pre-eminent sense. We do not just *respond* to visual stimuli: we *see* them as integral components of a visual world that has depth, substance and most important of all, a continuing existence separate from ourselves. It is through seeing that we gain most of our knowledge about external reality, and the possession of that knowledge, in turn, powerfully affects the way we see other things. In fact visual knowledge determines much of the basic content of our consciousness. Visual knowledge allows us to plan future actions, to picture the consequences of those actions, and to relive (sometimes with pleasure, sometimes with regret) what we have seen and done in the past. Vision affects the way we feel, as well as the way we think. Visual experiences can evoke powerful emotions, both positive and negative—as can the visual memories of what we have experienced before. Given the importance of vision in our mental life, it is not surprising that our language is full of visual metaphors. We can 'see the point', if we are not 'blind to the facts'; and occasionally show 'foresight' (though perhaps more often 'hindsight') by 'seeing the consequences' of our actions in our 'mind's eye'.

It is tempting to think that the delivery of such vivid experiences and the knowledge they impart is the entire raison d'être for vision. But the visual brain did not begin—in evolutionary terms—as a system designed to deliver conscious visual experience. That aspect of vision, while clearly extremely important, is a relative newcomer on the evolutionary landscape. So how did vision come on the scene originally?

To answer this question, we have to turn to evolutionary biology and ask: 'What is vision good for?' The answer from a biological point of view is quite straightforward. Vision evolved only because somehow improved an animal's fitness—in other words, proved its ability to survive and reproduce. Natural selection, differential survival of individuals in a population, ultimately nds on what animals *do* with the vision they have, not on they *experience*. It must have been the case therefore that vision began, in the mists of evolutionary time, as a way of guiding an organism's behavior. It was the practical effectiveness of our ancestors' behavior that shaped the ways our eyes and brains evolved. There was never any selection pressure for internal 'picture shows'—only for what vision could do in the service of external action. This is not to say that visual thinking, visual knowledge, and even visual experience did not arise through natural selection. But the only way this could have happened is through the benefits these mental processes have for behavior. Before returning to the intricacies of human vision, let us consider for a moment what kind of a role vision plays in the life of simpler organisms, which presumably do not have any mental life at all.

The origins of vision

A single-cell organism like the *Euglena*, which uses light as a source of energy, changes its pattern of swimming according to the different levels of illumination it encounters in its watery world. Such behavior keeps *Euglena* in regions of the environment where an important resource, sunlight, is available. But although this behavior is controlled by light, no one would seriously argue that the *Euglena* 'sees' the light or that it has some sort of internal model of the outside world. The simplest and most obvious way to understand this behavior is that it works as a simple reflex, translating light levels into changes in the rate and direction of swimming. Of course, a mechanism of this sort, although activated by light, is far less complicated than the visual systems of multicellular organisms. But even in complex organisms like vertebrates, many aspects of vision can be understood entirely as systems for controlling movement, without reference to perceptual experience or to any general-purpose representation of the outside world.

Vertebrates have a broad range of different visually guided behaviors. What is surprising is that these different patterns of activity are governed by quite independent visual control systems. The neurobiologist David Ingle, for example, showed during the

1970s that when frogs catch prey they use a quite separate visuo-motor control module from the one that guides them around visual obstacles blocking their path. These modules run on parallel tracks from the eye right through the brain to the motor output systems that execute the behavior. Ingle demonstrated the existence of these modules by taking advantage of the fact that nerves in the frog's brain, unlike those in the mammalian brain, can regenerate new connections when damaged. In his experiments, he was able to 'rewire' the visuomotor module for prey catching by first removing a structure called the optic tectum on one side. The optic nerves that brought information from the eye to the optic tectum on the damaged side of the brain were severed by this surgery. A few weeks later, however, the cut nerves re-grew, but finding their normal destination missing, crossed back over and connected with the remaining optic tectum on the other side of the brain. As a result, when these 'rewired' frogs were later tested with artificial prey objects, they turned and snapped their tongue to catch the prey—but in the opposite direction (see Figure 4.1). This

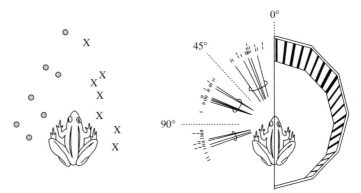

Figure 4.1

The dissociation between prey-catching behavior and visually-guided barrier avoidance in a 'rewired' frog. The drawing on the left shows that when a fake worm was presented to the eye opposite the missing optic tectum (at points shown by circles), the frog snapped at a mirror-image point on the other side (crosses). This is because the eye has become hooked up to the optic tectum on the wrong side of the brain. The optic tectum interprets the signals from this eye as if they were coming from the other eye (its usual source of visual input). The drawing on the right shows the directions in which the 'rewired' frog jumped in response to a gentle touch from behind in the presence of a barrier. The barrier was sometimes extended beyond the midline to positions 45° or 90° into the visual field of the rewired eye. A successful escape required the frog to turn and jump just enough to clear the edge of the barrier. The rewired frogs always cleared the barrier successfully, just like normal frogs. This is because only the eye's projections to the optic tectum were in fact rewired: the other projections, including those supporting barrier avoidance behavior, remained correctly hooked up. From Ingle, D.J. (1973). Two visual systems in the frog. *Science*, 181, 1053–1055 (Figures 1 & 2).

'mirror-imaged' behavior reflected the fact that the prey-catching system in these frogs was now wired up the wrong way around.

But this did not mean that their entire visual world was reversed. When Ingle tested the same frogs' ability to jump around a barrier blocking their route, their movements remained quite normal, even when the edge of the barrier was located in the same part of space where they made prey-catching errors (see Figure 4.1). It was as though the frogs saw the world correctly when skirting around a barrier, but saw the world mirror-imaged when snapping at prey. In fact, Ingle discovered that the optic nerves were still hooked up normally to a separate obstacle avoidance module in a part of the brain quite separate from the optic tectum. This part of the brain, which sits just in front of optic tectum, is called the pretectum. Ingle was subsequently able to selectively rewire the pretectum in another group of frogs. These animals jumped right into an obstacle placed in front of them instead of avoiding it, yet still continued to show normal prey catching.

What did these rewired frogs 'see'? There is no sensible answer to this. The question only makes sense if you believe that the brain has a single visual representation of the outside world that governs all of an animal's behavior. Ingle's experiments reveal that this cannot possibly be true. Once you accept that there are separate visuomotor modules in the brain of the frog, the puzzle disappears. We now know that there are at least five separate visuomotor modules in the brains of frogs and toads, each looking after a different kind of visually guided behavior and each having distinct input and output pathways. Obviously the outputs of these different modules have to be coordinated, but in no sense are they all guided by a single visual representation of the world residing somewhere in the frog's brain.

The same kind of visuomotor 'modularity' exists in mammals. Evidence for this can be seen even in the anatomy of the visual system. As Box 4.1 makes clear, the retina sends its optic nerve fibers to a number of different sites in the brain. Each of these brain structures in turn gives rise to a distinctive set of outgoing connections. The existence of these separate input–output lines in the mammalian brain suggests that they may each be responsible for controlling a different kind of behavior—in much the same way as they are in the frog. The mammalian brain is more

Box 4.1   Routes from the eye to the brain

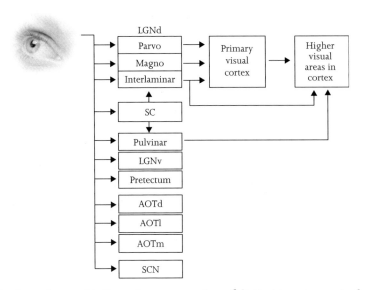

Neurons in the retina send information to a number of distinct target areas in the brain. The two largest pathways from the eye to the brain in humans and other mammals are the ones projecting to the superior colliculus (SC) and the dorsal part of the lateral geniculate nucleus in the thalamus (LGNd). The pathway to the SC is a much more ancient system (in the evolutionary sense) and is the most prominent pathway in other vertebrates such as amphibians, reptiles, and birds. The SC (or optic tectum, as it is called in non-mammalian animals) is a layered structure forming the roof (Latin: *tectum*) of the midbrain. It is interconnected with a large number of other brain structures, including motor nuclei in the brainstem and spinal cord. It also sends inputs to a number of different sites in the cerebral cortex. The SC appears to play an essential role in the control of the rapid eye and head movements that animals make toward important or interesting objects in their visual world.

The pathway to the LGNd is the most prominent visual pathway in humans and other higher mammals. Neurons in the primate LGNd project in turn to the cerebral cortex, with almost all of the fibers ending up in the primary visual area, or striate cortex (often nowadays termed area V1) in the occipital lobe. This set of projections and its cortical elaborations probably constitute the best-studied neural system in the whole of neuroscience. Scientists' fascination with the so-called 'geniculo– striate' pathway is related to the fact that our subjective experience of the world depends on the integrity of this projection system (see the section on 'Blindsight' in Chapter 5).

Although the projections to the SC and LGNd are the most prominent visual pathways in the human brain, there are a number of other retinal pathways that are not nearly so well studied as the first two. One of the earliest pathways to leave the optic nerve consists of a small bundle of fibers that project to the so-called suprachiasmatic nucleus (SCN). The visual inputs to the SCN are important for synchronizing our biorhythms with the day–night cycle.

There are also projections to the ventral portion of the lateral geniculate nucleus (LGNv), the pulvinar nucleus and various pretectal nuclei, and a set of three nuclei in the brainstem known collectively as the nuclei of the accessory optic tract (AOT). The different functions of these various projections are not yet well understood—although they appear to play a critical role in the mediation of a number of 'automatic' reactions to visual stimuli. The AOT have been implicated in the visual control of posture and certain aspects of locomotion, and have been shown to be sensitive to the optic flow on the retina that is created as we move through the world. The AOT also plays an important role in controlling the alternating fast and slow eye movements that we make when looking at a large visual stimulus, such as a train, passing before our eyes. Retinal projections to one area in the pretectum are thought to be part of the circuitry controlling the pupillary light reflex—the constriction of the pupil as we move into a brightly lit environment such as that found on the beach or the ski slopes. There is also some evidence from studies in amphibians and lower mammals that certain pretectal nuclei play a role in visually guided obstacle avoidance during locomotion. However almost nothing is known about the functions of the other pretectal nuclei, the ventral part of the lateral geniculate nucleus, or the pulvinar.

complex than that of the frog, but the same principles of modularity still seem to apply. In rats and gerbils, for example, orientation movements of the head and eyes toward morsels of food are served by brain circuits that are quite separate from those dealing with obstacles that need to be avoided while the animal is running around. In fact, these brain circuits in the mammal are directly homologous to the circuits we have already mentioned in frogs and toads, reflecting a common ancestry. For example, the circuit controlling orientation movements of the head and eyes in rats and gerbils involves the optic tectum (or superior colliculus as it is called in mammals), the same structure in the frog that controls turning and snapping the tongue at flies.

The fact that each part of the animal's behavioral repertoire has its own separate visual control system refutes the common assumption that all behavior is controlled by a single general-purpose representation of the visual world. Instead, it seems, vision evolved, not as a single system that allowed organisms to 'see' the world, but as an expanding collection of relatively independent visuomotor modules.

Vision for perception

Of course, in complex animals such as humans and other primates, such as monkeys, vision has evolved beyond a set of discrete visuomotor modules. Much of our own behavior is certainly not rigidly bound by our sensory input. Even frogs can learn to some degree from their previous visual encounters with the world—but humans and other higher primates can use their previous visual experience and knowledge of the visual world in much more flexible ways so as to guide what they do in the future. We can internally rehearse different courses of action, for example, often using visual imagery in doing so, before deciding what to do.

In other words, vision can serve action not just in the here and now, but also 'off-line'—at other times and in other places. To do this, the visual brain creates a rich and detailed representation of the visual scene that the animal is looking at. We do not know what animals experience, but in humans at least, these perceptual representations are normally conscious. We experience them, and thereby we can communicate them to others. The visual mechanisms that generate these representations are quite different from the simple visuomotor modules of amphibians described earlier, and appear to have arisen more recently in evolutionary time. Rather than being linked directly to specific motor outputs, these new mechanisms create a perceptual representation that can be used for many different purposes. Moreover, as we mentioned in Chapter 1, our perception of the world is not slavishly driven by the pattern of light on the eye but is also shaped by our memories, emotions, and expectations. Visuomotor mechanisms may be driven largely bottom-up but perception has an important top-down component as well. The memories that affect our perception in this top-down way are themselves built up from previous perceptions. As a result of all this two-way traffic, perception and memory literally blend into one another. After all, we have visual experiences in our dreams, and these must be generated entirely by top-down processes derived from memory.

These general-purpose representations confer a big advantage in that they allow us to choose a goal, plan ahead, and decide upon a course of action. But on the other hand they do not have any direct contact with the motor system. The on-line visual control of our actions still remains the responsibility of dedicated visuomotor modules that are similar in principle to those found in frogs and toads.

It is important to bear in mind that when people talk about what they 'see', they are talking only about the products of their perceptual system. Yet until recently researchers on vision have seen no need to go further than perceptual reports when gathering their data. In fact, a very important tradition in visual research, called psychophysics, depends entirely on what people report about what they can and cannot see. It has always been assumed that this is all there is to vision. Admittedly, psychophysics, which was founded by the nineteenth-century German physicist turned philosopher, Gustav Fechner, has told us a great deal about the capacities and limits of the perceptual system. But it has told us nothing about how vision controls the skilled movements that we make. The reason that psychophysics has failed in this regard is because the visuomotor machinery governing our actions is simply not accessible to conscious report. We may have a conscious visual experience of a coffee cup in front of us, but this experience will tell us little about the particular visual information that enables us to pick up the cup.

Vision for action

Alongside the evolution of perceptual systems in the brains of higher mammals such as humans, the visuomotor systems in turn have become progressively more complex. The main reason for this is that the movements we make have themselves become more complex. In our primate ancestors, one of the great landmarks in evolution was the emergence of the prehensile hand—a device that is capable of grasping objects and manipulating them with great dexterity. But just as the development of any sophisticated piece of machinery, such as an industrial robot, needs an equally sophisticated computer to control it, the evolution of the primate hand would have been useless without the coevolution of an equally intricate control system. The control of eye movements too has become more sophisticated and has become closely linked with the control of our hand movements. All of these changes, in other words, were accompanied by the evolution of new brain circuitry. Many of these new control systems in the brain have strong links to and from the basic modules in those older parts of the brain that were already present in simpler vertebrates like frogs and toads.

A good example of the way that these connections operate can be seen in the control of rapid (saccadic) eye movements in primates, such as monkeys and humans. We have seen already that head and eye movements in rodents are controlled by the same basic structures (the optic tectum, or superior colliculus) that control prey-catching in frogs. These same structures retain a central role in the machinery that programs head and eye movements in primates. But now these ancient visuomotor circuits have become subject to regulation and refinement by newer brain structures, where more intricate computations can be brought into play.

At first sight this may seem a puzzle—why didn't nature devise totally new systems from the ground up? In his book *Evolving Brains*, the American neurobiologist John Allman tells the story of how, on a visit to a power generation plant during the 1970s, he was struck by the side by side coexistence of several control systems for the generators dating from different periods in the life of the plant. There were pneumatic controls and a system of controls based on vacuum tube technology, along with several generations of computer-based control systems. All of these systems were being used to control the processes of electrical generation at the plant. When he asked the reason for this strange mix, he was told that the demand for power had always been too great for the plant ever to be shut down. As Allman points out:

> The brain has evolved in the same manner as the control systems in this power plant. The brain, like the power plant, can never be shut down and fundamentally reconfigured, even between generations. All the old control systems must remain in place, and new ones with additional capacities are added and integrated in such a way as to enhance survival.

It seems, however, that while these expanded visuomotor systems in higher mammals govern much more complex behaviors, they remain essentially automatic and are no more accessible to consciousness than those in the frog (or the *Euglena* for that matter). They might carry out more sophisticated and subtle computations on the visual information they receive, but they can do this perfectly well without a visual representation of the world. In fact, these visuomotor networks no more need conscious representations of the world than does an industrial robot. The primary role of perceptual representations is not in the *execution* of actions, but rather in helping the person or animal to arrive at a decision to act in a particular way.

As we shall now see in the last section of this chapter, there has been a massive expansion in primates of the areas devoted to visual processing in the most prominent part of the mammalian brain—the cerebral cortex. We can understand this development by seeing it as reflecting the two closely related developments that we have outlined above. One development is the emergence of *perceptual systems* for identifying objects in the visual world and attaching meaning and significance to them. And the other is the emergence of more complex *visuomotor control systems* that permit the execution of skilled actions directed at those objects.

The sites of sight: Two visual streams in the primate cortex

In 1982 a seminal article appeared in the literature that has been cited more frequently than any other paper in the field of visual neuroscience, before or since. It was called 'Two cortical visual systems' and was written by two eminent American neuroscientists, Leslie Ungerleider and Mort Mishkin. They summarized converging experimental evidence mostly derived from monkeys, whose visual brains and visual abilities are closely similar to ours. Signals from the eyes first arrive at the cerebral cortex (the outer shell of gray matter that forms the evolutionary pinnacle of the brain) in a small area at the back called the primary visual area (V1). Ungerleider and Mishkin argued convincingly that the signals were then routed forwards along two quite separate pathways within the cortex (see Figure 4.2). One of these routes, which they called the dorsal visual pathway, ended up in part of the brain at the top of the cerebral hemispheres, the posterior parietal region. The other (the so-called ventral visual pathway) ended up at the bottom and sides of the hemispheres, in the inferior temporal region. These two pathways are now often called the dorsal and ventral *streams* of visual processing.

Many more visual areas have been discovered in the last twenty years and as a result there is a far more complicated pattern of interconnections than anyone thought possible back in 1982 (see Plate 2, bottom). Nevertheless, the basic wiring plan

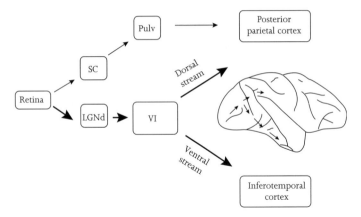

Figure 4.2
A schematic diagram of Ungerleider and Mishkin's original (1982) model of the two streams of visual processing in primate cerebral cortex. The brain illustrated is that of an Old World monkey. The ventral stream receives most of its visual input from the primary visual cortex (V1), which in turn receives its input from the lateral geniculate nucleus (LGNd) of the thalamus. The dorsal stream also receives input from V1, but in addition gets a substantial input from the superior colliculus (SC) via the pulvinar (Pulv), another nucleus in the thalamus. From Milner, A.D. & Goodale, M.A. (1995). Visual Brain in Action, Oxford University Press (Figure 3.1).

first identified by Ungerleider and Mishkin still stands: a dorsal stream going to the posterior parietal cortex and a ventral stream going to the inferior temporal cortex. What is remarkable is that the division of labor between these two information highways in the monkey's brain appears to map rather nicely onto the distinction we have been making between 'vision for action' and 'vision for perception' in humans.

The evidence for this mapping comes from two complementary kinds of research. First, there is evidence from lesion experiments, in which the dorsal and ventral streams in monkeys have been separately damaged to see what effects this damage might have on different kinds of visual behavior. Second, there is evidence from single-cell recording, in which the kinds of visual information that are encoded in individual nerve cells (neurons) can be monitored.

Doing without one stream

Studying how brain damage affects behavior in animals has had a long history. Even in mid-Victorian times, experimentally minded neurologists had begun to make selective lesions of brain tissue in animals, in the hope of gaining some understanding of the many brain-damaged people entering their clinics. The Scottish neurologist David Ferrier was a pioneer in this field. During the 1860s, he removed most of what we now call the dorsal stream in a monkey, and discovered that it would mis-reach and fumble for food items set out in front of it. In a similar vein, work by Mitch Glickstein in England has shown that small lesions in the dorsal stream can make a monkey unable to pry food morsels out of narrow slots set at different orientations. The monkey is far from blind, but it cannot use vision to insert its finger and thumb at the right angle to get the food. It eventually does it by touch, but its initial efforts, under visual guidance, fail. Yet these same monkeys had no difficulty in telling apart different visual patterns, including lines of different orientation. These observations and a host of others have demonstrated that dorsal stream damage in the monkey results in very similar abilities and disabilities to those we saw in Ruth Vickers and Anne Thiérry. In other words, monkeys with dorsal-stream lesions show major problems in vision for action but evidently not in vision for perception.

In direct contrast, Heinrich Klüver and Paul Bucy, working at the University of Chicago in the 1930s, found that monkeys with lesions of the temporal lobes, including what we now know as the ventral stream, did not have any visuomotor problems at all, but did have difficulties in recognizing familiar objects, and in learning to distinguish between new ones. Klüver and Bucy referred to these problems as symptoms of 'visual agnosia', and indeed they do look very like the problems that Dee Fletcher has. Moreover, like Dee, these monkeys with ventral-stream lesions had no problem using their vision to pick up small objects. The influential neuroscientist, Karl Pribram, once noted that monkeys with ventral-stream lesions that had been trained for months to no avail to distinguish between simple visual patterns, would sit in their cages snatching flies out of the air with great dexterity. Mitch Glickstein recently confirmed that such monkeys do indeed retain excellent visuomotor skills. He found that monkeys with ventral-stream damage had no problem at all using their finger and thumb to retrieve food items embedded in narrow slots— quite unlike his monkeys with dorsal-stream lesions.

Eavesdropping on neurons in the brain

By the 1950s physiologists had devised methods for recording the electrical activity of individual neurons in the living

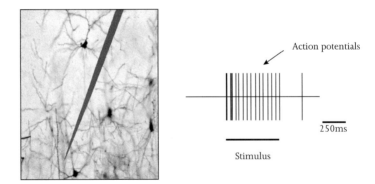

Figure 4.3

The photograph shows the tip of a microelectrode superimposed on a stained
section of brain tissue, to show the relative size of the electrode in relation to typical
neurons. (In reality the neurons would be much more densely packed than shown
here, since only a minority of cells show up using this particular kind of histological
stain.) Alongside the photograph is a diagram representing a train of action
potentials recorded by such a microelectrode when the adjacent neuron is activated
by a suitable visual stimulus.

brain (see Figure 4.3). The American Nobel Laureates David Hubel
and Torsten Wiesel used these techniques to study the visual system, and found in the late 1950s that neurons in primary visual
cortex (area V1) would 'fire' (i.e. give a small electrical response)
every time a visual edge or line was shown to the eye, so long as
it was shown at the right orientation and in the right location
within the field of view. They discovered, in other words, that
these neurons are 'encoding' the orientation and position of particular edges that make up a visual scene out there in the world.
Different neurons prefer (or are 'tuned' to) different orientations
of edges (see Figure 4.4). Other neurons are tuned for the colors
of objects, and still others code the direction in which an object
is moving. The distribution of these neurons within primary
visual cortex is not haphazard. Neurons tuned to a particular orientation, for example, are clustered together in columns which
run through the depth of the cortex. When Hubel and Wiesel
explored visual areas beyond primary visual cortex, they found
neurons that coded for more complicated visual features.

The 1960s and early 1970s heralded great advances in single-
cell recording as investigators pushed well beyond the early visual
areas, out into the dorsal and ventral streams. It soon became
apparent that neurons in the two streams coded the visual world
very differently.

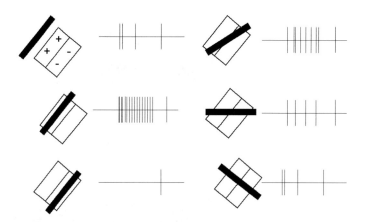

Figure 4.4

A diagram illustrating a neuron in area V1 that responds selectively to the orientation at which an edge or bar is shown to a monkey. The rectangle marks the location in space where the bar has to be presented for the neuron to respond (the neuron's receptive field). The plus signs indicate a region of the receptive field where presenting a small stimulus will result in an increase in the firing of the neuron. The negative signs indicate a region where presenting a small stimulus will result in a decrease in firing. This means that the orientation of the bar is critical in determining the firing rate of the neuron. Other neurons will have their receptive fields organized differently and thus will 'prefer' a different orientation of the bar.

The first person to probe the inferior temporal cortex, deep in the ventral stream, was Charles Gross at Princeton University. He found that neurons here were not satisfied with simple lines and edges, but needed to 'see' much more complex visual patterns before they would fire. In fact some neurons were so specific that they remained 'silent' until a hand or a face was shown to the monkey (see Figure 4.5). Keiji Tanaka, a neuroscientist working in Tokyo, has found clusters of neurons in inferior temporal cortex analogous to those previously found in area V1—only this time the neurons do not share a simple preference like 45°-oriented edges; they share a preference for a particular complex pattern of features.

Although the neurons in the ventral stream are quite fussy about the kind of object they respond to, a good number of them are not at all fussy about the particular viewpoint from which the object is seen or even where it is within the field of view. The neurons are also largely oblivious to the lighting conditions or the distance of the object from the eye. Neurons with these characteristics are exactly what is needed to identify a particular object across a wide range of viewing conditions—the kind of neurons that one would expect to see in a pathway specialized for perception.

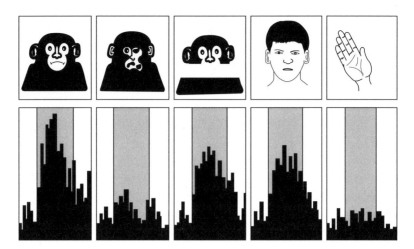

Figure 4.5
An example of a 'face cell' recorded within the ventral stream of a monkey's brain.
This particular cell responded well to pictures of human or monkey faces seen in full
front view, but less well when the picture was jumbled or when other objects such as
a hand were shown to the monkey. The responses of the neuron are shown in the
graphs below each image. The gray area on each graph shows the time over which
the picture of the face or other object was shown to the monkey.

The next important development was in the mid-1970s, when
scientists began to record from visual neurons in the dorsal
stream. Working independently, Vernon Mountcastle at Johns
Hopkins University and Juhani Hyvärinen in Helsinki, Finland,
were the first to explore the properties of these neurons in detail.
The surprising thing about neurons deep in the dorsal stream is
the fact that although they are visually responsive, most of them
fire strongly only when the monkey actually responds in some
way to the visual target. For example, some neurons fire only
when the monkey reaches out toward a target; others require that
the monkey flick their eyes (i.e. make saccades) toward a stationary target; and still others fire to a moving target but only if the
monkey follows it with its eyes. A particularly fascinating group of
neurons, which were studied in detail during the 1990s by Hideo
Sakata and his colleagues in Tokyo, respond when the monkey
grasps or manipulates a target of a particular shape and orientation (see Figure 4.6).

These different subsets of neurons are clustered in somewhat
separate regions of the posterior parietal cortex, with the 'grasp
neurons', for example, located mostly toward the front end of the

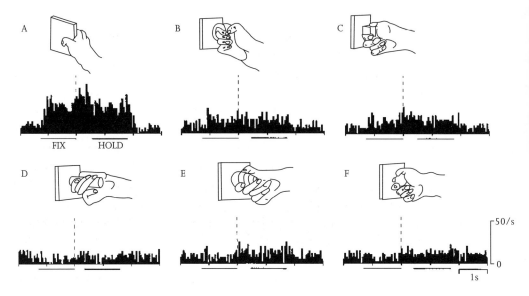

Figure 4.6

The activity of a neuron in area AIP when a monkey looks at and then grasps six different kinds of solid shapes. As the graphs below each shape show, the neuron responds best when the monkey grasps a vertically-oriented square plate. The neuron begins to fire when the monkey is first shown the object (marked 'fix' for fixation) and continues to fire after the monkey has grasped it (marked 'hold'). From Murata, A., Gallese, V., Luppino, G., Kaseda, M., & Sakata, H. (2000). Selectivity for the shape, size, and orientation of objects for grasping in neurons of monkey parietal AIP. *Journal of Neurophysiology*, 83, 2580–2601 (Figure 4).

region (area AIP). But despite their differences, what most of these neurons in the dorsal stream have in common is that they do not fire unless the monkey not only sees an object but in some way acts upon it as well. These are just the sorts of neurons you would expect to see in a 'vision for action' pathway.

Where do the two pathways lead?

The evidence reviewed above suggests that the ventral stream of visual processing in the monkey is the main conduit for transforming visual signals into perception whereas the dorsal stream plays the critical role in transforming visual signals into action. This division of labor is reflected in the outputs of the two visual pathways.

Consider the dorsal stream first. As we mentioned earlier, the behavioral repertoire of primates is much broader than that of the frog or even the gerbil. Fine hand and finger movements in particular imposed new demands on the visual system, and the evolutionary development of the dorsal stream can be seen as a response to these demands. It is no accident that the visuomotor areas in the posterior parietal cortex sit right next to the cortical areas that get tactile information from the hand and arm. These visuomotor areas are also intimately linked with parts of the motor cortex in the frontal lobe that send commands to the lower parts of the brain and the spinal cord. In fact, there are also direct pathways from the dorsal stream to lower parts of the brain, such as the superior colliculus, and to other way-stations that send instructions to the eye muscles and to parts of the spinal cord that control the limbs.

The ventral stream has none of these direct connections with motor systems. Instead, as befitting its role in perception and recognition, it interfaces with structures in the temporal and frontal lobes that have been implicated in memory, emotion and social behavior. It is especially interesting, in the light of what we said earlier about the role of memory in perception, that these connections are very much two-way. Yet ultimately the perceptual system has to influence behavior. If it didn't, we wouldn't have one! The difference from the dorsal stream is that the ventral stream connections with the motor systems producing the behavior are by their very nature highly indirect. In fact, the connections can never be fully specified since the range of behavior that perception can influence is essentially infinite.

Summary

Vision serves behavior, but it does so in a variety of direct and indirect ways. What we can learn from studying animals other than ourselves is that there is not just one way of seeing, because we see for so many different purposes. Just as there is no sense in asking what David Ingle's frogs 'see', it is important to realize that in many contexts it will make no sense to ask ourselves the same question. We are aware of what one of our visual systems tells us about the world, because we are privy to its products—but there remains a whole realm of visual processing that we can never experience or reflect on. We are certainly aware of the actions that these visuomotor systems control, but we have no direct experience of the visual information they use.

Streams within streams

The building blocks of perception

Dee Fletcher is not blind. She even has a good deal of visual phenomenology: in other words she still *perceives* certain aspects of the world. Dee continues to enjoy vivid and distinct experiences of color, for example, and can appreciate the fine detail of the surfaces of objects. This allows her still to take pleasure in looking at (and surprisingly often, identifying) the blossoms and foliage of different plants and trees as she walks through her garden or is driven through the countryside. At the same time though, she cannot recognize objects on the basis of their shape alone. As we saw earlier, she cannot recognize black and white drawings of objects that she could identify on the basis of their color or visual texture. The incomplete visual world that Dee lives in strongly suggests that the parts of the brain that are responsible for delivering our experiences of color and of form are different and separate from each other—and that only the part that deals with form perception has been damaged in her case. If so, then it would be expected that brain damage could occasionally cause the opposite pattern, causing a loss of color experience with a retained ability to recognize and distinguish different shapes.

As it turns out, this pattern of visual loss does sometimes occur. Individuals with this problem, known as 'cerebral achromatopsia', have a special form of color blindness in which the color-sensitive cones in the eye are all working normally but the apparatus in the brain that provides the experience of color is damaged. Strange as it may seem, individuals who have developed achromatopsia are often able to see the borders between two equally bright colors, say red and green, even though they are completely unable to say which side is red and which side is green!

Achromatopsia is not a color-naming problem. An individual with achromatopsia can tell you that bananas are yellow yet when asked to color in a line drawing of a banana is just as likely to use the blue or red crayon as the yellow one. They sometimes describe seeing the world in various shades of gray. Dee has at least been spared this understandably depressing kind of experience, which is described graphically in Oliver Sacks's essay 'The case of the color-blind painter' in his well-known book 'An Anthropologist on Mars'.

The contrast between Dee's visual experience and that of an achromatopsic patient provides another example of a double dissociation, an idea that we introduced in Chapter 3. Then, however, we were concerned to distinguish between just two broad categories of visual processing—one devoted to delivering our perceptions, the other to guiding our actions. We noted that each of those functions could be separately and independently disrupted by brain damage. But even within just one of those broad categories—that of perception—there are double dissociations as well. So although you may think that you see a single integrated representation of a visual scene, like an image on a movie screen, your brain is actually analyzing different aspects of the scene separately using different visual 'modules'. The products of these modules may never be combined into a single 'picture' in the brain—even though those outputs have to be cross-referenced or bound together in some way. After all, the brain has to be able to distinguish between a red pepper on a green plate and a green pepper on a red plate.

Of course colors and shapes are very basic and ubiquitous features of our visual experience, features that we use to distinguish among most of the things we know in everyday life—man-made objects, animals, plants, major landmarks, other people. But the brain also seems to channel visual information into more specialized recognition systems as well, and damage to these can produce quite specific recognition difficulties. Perhaps the best-known example of this is the condition known as 'prosopagnosia' (from the Greek prosopon, meaning person). An individual who suffers from this problem may be quite unable to recognize even a close member of their family, or a famous personality, when all they have to go on is the person's face. They generally have no difficulty when they hear the person speak, or even when they see the person moving around in habitual ways. Of course there are many aspects of a face that our brains take into account when we recognize a person: skin coloration and texture, hair color and hairline, facial shape, and the placement of features like the eyes and mouth. Nonetheless it is striking that a person with prosopagnosia typically does not have a general agnosia for objects. It is just faces they have a problem with. Perhaps more remarkably, a recent study by Morris Moscovitch and his colleagues in Toronto has documented the case of a man, Charles K., whose brain damage has caused the opposite pattern—a devastating loss in the ability to recognize objects without any problem in recognizing faces (see Plate 3). This fascinating case provides us with yet another double dissociation: 'faces lost, objects intact' in one person; 'faces intact, objects lost' in the other.

So we can see that there is modularity in the ventral stream on at least two levels. We see it first at the level of primitive visual features (color, edges, motion), which are processed by quite separate systems. But these modules do not then simply join together to feed into a general-purpose object recognition system. Rather, these lower-level channels evidently feed their information into *multiple* higher-level systems, each specialized for a particular category of things in the world. (see also Box 5.2.)

Faces seem to constitute a unique class of stimuli for human beings. In social animals such as monkeys and humans, in which the recognition of individuals plays a critical role in everyday interactions, the ability to identify faces is a hugely important skill. So relevant are faces to our daily lives that we often imagine that we see them in places where they do not exist, for example on the surface of the moon. The identification of faces takes place in a rapid, holistic way rather than in a feature-by-feature fashion. Thus, for example, we can detect family resemblances between individuals without being able to point to how we do it. (For another example of the specialized nature of face recognition, see Plate 5, top.)

But faces are not the only category of special objects that have their own dedicated hardware in the brain which when damaged results in a specific agnosia. Another, less well known, example of a specific agnosia is one where a person loses the ability to find their way around a once-familiar environment, such as their hometown. This so-called 'topographical agnosia' can in many cases be attributed to a loss of recognition for particular major landmarks, such as a street corner church or pub. We generally use landmarks of these kinds in orienting ourselves and in constructing an internal map of our environment. While this difficulty is often associated with prosopagnosia, each can occur without the other. This implies that the two visual problems result from damage to two different specialized mechanisms that happen to lie close together in the brain. Of course not all patients have their recognition difficulties restricted to single domain, as in prosopagnosia or topographical agnosia. Dee Fletcher, for example, is herself prosopagnosic, in addition to having, like Moscovitch's patient Charles K., a severe object agnosia.

These inferences from clinical observations have been reinforced in recent years by a number of functional brain imaging studies, in which healthy people view pictures or objects of different kinds, while the activation pattern in their brains (generally as inferred from the changes in blood flow through the vessels that supply the brain) is measured (see Box 5.1). These studies allow us not only to 'look inside the heads' of brain-damaged people to determine where their damage is located, but also to eavesdrop inside the heads of undamaged individuals to map which areas change their activity when the person sees or does particular things. For example, Semir Zeki and his collaborators in University College London, discovered some years ago that an abstract Mondrian-style pattern made up of different-colored patches activates a different set of cortical areas than a comparable pattern made up only of shades of gray. When the two activation maps were subtracted from each other, a particular part of the brain could be seen to be selectively associated with viewing the colored pattern. Gratifyingly, this 'color area' corresponds closely to the area where damage causes achromatopsia.

Similar functional imaging studies have confirmed the existence of separate areas dedicated respectively to the perception of faces and places. For example, Nancy Kanwisher at MIT has identified a 'face area' which she named FFA (fusiform face area), which is activated much more by pictures of faces than by other pictures such as everyday objects, buildings, or even scrambled pictures of faces (see Plate 4, top). This area is quite separate from another area (PPA—parahippocampal place area) which is activated by pictures of buildings and scenes, but much less by faces. Yet another area has been identified which relates to everyday objects (like fruit, cups,

Box 5.1   Functional neuroimaging

The development of new imaging techniques has enabled scientists to pinpoint the activity of different regions of the brain with considerable accuracy. One of the first techniques to be developed was positron emission tomography (PET). In PET studies, a radioactively labeled substance or 'tracer' is introduced either by injection or by having the subject inhale the radioactive substance. The amount of radiation involved is extremely small and does not constitute any danger to the individual.

In one version of PET, the person inhales oxygen that has been radioactively labeled and the labeled oxygen is then absorbed into the blood. Because blood flow increases in areas of the brain that are active, these differences in regional cerebral blood flow (rCBF) can be localized by detecting the positrons emitted by the radioactive oxygen in the blood using an array of scintillation counters placed around the person's head.

In another version of PET, a radioactively labeled substance such as 2-deoxyglucose (2-DG) is injected into the blood. 2-DG is a variety of glucose that once absorbed into a cell cannot be broken down like normal glucose. This means that active neurons in the brain will absorb 2-DG along with the regular glucose that they need as fuel—but the 2-DG will accumulate in the neurons. Again using scintillation counters the number of positrons emitted by the radioactively labeled 2-DG can be measured—and the degree of activity in different brain regions can be localized.

Although PET studies have revealed a good deal about the functional organization of the human brain, the technique does have limitations. First, the spatial resolution of PET is quite coarse; it cannot resolve regions any smaller than about 1 cm^3. Second, because radioactive substances have to be injected or inhaled, only a limited number of brain scans can be carried out on a single person. Finally, it is quite expensive—mainly because a cyclotron has to be used to create the radioactively labeled material.

A newer brain imaging technique, functional magnetic resonance imaging (fMRI) has overtaken PET as the main method for imaging functional activity in the human brain. Functional MRI has better spatial resolution (up to 1 mm^3 or better), is much less expensive, and does not require anything to be injected into the person whose brain is being scanned. In fact, because it is so safe, people can be scanned many times. fMRI is an adaptation of an earlier technique called magnetic resonance imaging (or MRI) in which the three-dimensional structure of the brain can be visualized using high magnetic fields.

To make an MRI of the brain, the person's head is placed inside a strong magnetic field (as much as 80,000 times more powerful than the earth's magnetic field). The atoms in the hydrogen molecules in the person's brain tissue align with that magnetic field (a bit like a compass needle aligning with the earth's magnetic field). A short pulse of radiofrequency energy is then administered to the brain causing the alignment of the hydrogen atoms to be perturbed. As the atoms return to their original alignment in the magnetic field, they give off tiny amounts of energy that can be detected by an antenna or 'receiver' coil placed around the head. Because the density of water (and thus hydrogen atoms) varies systematically between the gray and white matter of the brain (i.e., between the cell bodies and the connecting fibers), the three-dimensional anatomical structure of the brain can be reconstructed based on the differences in the strength of the signals generated by different kinds of brain tissue.

Functional MRI exploits the fact that oxygenated blood has different magnetic properties from deoxygenated blood. Hydrogen molecules that are in the vicinity of oxygenated blood in active brain areas give off a slightly different signal from hydrogen molecules near deoxygenated blood. The receiver coil picks up the blood oxygen level dependent (BOLD) signals, which reflect increased activity of neurons in particular brain areas. The BOLD signals measured when a person performs one task in the magnet can be compared to the BOLD signals that are measured when the person performs another task. The difference between these BOLD signals can then be mapped onto a detailed structural MRI of the brain—revealing patterns of activity that are correlated with the performance of one kind of task but not another.

TV sets, and vases). This region, generally called the lateral occipital area (or area LO) is revealed by taking fMRI scans while people look either at pictures of intact objects or at scrambled pictures of objects, and then subtracting the two scan images. This subtraction removes the brain activation caused just by the constituent lines and edges, leaving behind the activity related specifically to the structure present in the intact pictures (see Plate 8, top). The critical areas for colors, faces, and places are located close together on the underside of the brain near the junction of the occipital and temporal lobes, combining to form a region, along with area LO, more on the lateral surface, that constitutes most of the human equivalent of the monkey's ventral stream. Although the degree of overlap among the different areas remains controversial, there is no doubting their separate existence. The brain imaging experiments and the clinical studies both point to one undeniable conclusion: our perceptual experience is not the product of a general purpose object recognition system but is instead the creation of a set of quasi-independent visual modules.

This cluster of visual areas on the underside of the temporal lobes seems to house most of the machinery that underlies our perceptual experience. Not all disorders of perception are linked to this brain region however. One particular selective loss, sometimes known as akinetopsia, is associated with damage to a quite different part of the brain. In this very rare condition, the patient loses the ability to see motion. An individual with akinetopsia will be able to see stationary objects perfectly well, but will soon lose track of any object that is moving relatively quickly. For example, the neuropsychologist Josef Zihl described a patient living in Munich who had difficulty pouring coffee into a cup, because she could not see the level of the liquid rising—she saw it as a series of stationary snapshots instead. She sometimes experienced an everyday scene as being filled with jerky movements rather as if it were stroboscopically illuminated, or as if she were watching an old silent movie. Crossing the street was a nightmare for her. At one moment, a car would be some distance away and the next moment it would have jumped right in front of her. She never saw it moving.

Interestingly, while many cases have been described of patients whose brain damage has caused combinations of prosopagnosia, achromatopsia, and topographical agnosia, these disorders are almost never seen in combination with akinetopsia. The reason for this is more geographical than functional. As can be seen in the brain map shown in Plate 4, top, the layout of the visual areas that deal with faces, colors and places all lie in close proximity to each other on the underside of the brain, so that damage to one is quite likely to impinge on one or more of the other areas. In contrast, the 'motion area' lies some way away, still within the temporal lobe, but up above area LO on the side of the brain. This area was first identified in the monkey over thirty years ago by Semir Zeki, who showed that it gets direct inputs from area V1. Zeki went on to show that individual neurons in this area (which he called V5, though it is now usually called MT) would fire only when a moving visual spot was shown to the monkey in a particular part of its visual field. Moreover, the spot not only had to be moving but had to be going in a certain direction at a certain speed. What did not matter, however was the color, shape, or visual texture of the moving spot.

To cut a long story short, the clinical observations of patients with selective visual deficits fit well with what we know from many years of detailed study of the visual areas in the monkey's brain and with the exciting developments that we now see

63

unfolding in the field of human brain imaging. It turns out, for example, that the functional maps of the ventral stream in monkey and human are strikingly similar in their layout, especially when the cortex is artificially flattened to show the visual areas that are buried in the fissures (sometimes called 'sulci') of the brain (see Plate 2, bottom).

The building blocks of visually guided action

Just as there is modularity in the ventral stream, so there is also modularity in the dorsal stream. But the modularity in the dorsal stream is based not on the particular visual features that are being extracted from the visual array so much as on the nature of the actions guided by vision. These actions include things like reaching; saccadic (quick) eye movements; pursuit (slow) eye movements; grasping with the hand and whole-body locomotion. Of course these elementary actions rarely occur in isolation in everyday behavior. Instead, they are combined in an infinite number of different ways to serve our behavioral needs. For example, to pick up a coffee cup from the table, we might walk toward the table, turn our eyes to the cup, extend our hand toward it, simultaneously configuring the posture of fingers in readiness to grasp the handle, and then finally grasp it and pick it up. These different action elements would never be put together in exactly the same way on two different occasions. In fact, each element would have to be individually guided by different visual information. So although there must be some kind of overall orchestration of the different elements of the action, each also needs its own visual guidance system. This need for separate guidance systems has led to the evolution of separate visuo-motor modules in the posterior parietal cortex, each of which is responsible for the visual control of a particular class of movements.

These different visuomotor areas in the parietal cortex are linked with similarly dedicated regions within part of the frontal lobe known as pre-motor cortex. In other words, the dorsal stream's modules are probably better described as parieto-frontal modules. As mentioned in the last chapter, these modules also link up with sensorimotor control structures (like the pons, superior colliculus, and cerebellum) in the lower, more ancient parts of the brain. These structures are dedicated to the production of elementary eye or limb movements whose output parameters are tightly specified. As we suggested in Chapter 4, the newer parieto-frontal modules can be regarded as constituting a high-level 'managerial' system, which provides flexible control over these older and more 'reflexive' visuomotor networks in the brainstem.

Just as was the case for the ventral stream, the evidence for separate and specialized dorsal stream modules in humans came initially from clinical studies of patients with lesions in localized regions of the cerebral cortex. The classic Bálint syndrome (as exemplified by Ruth Vickers and Anne Thiérry) is characterized by a host of visuomotor disabilities, ranging from difficulties in making saccadic eye movements through to problems with visually guided reaching and grasping. Of course, in these patients the lesions are typically quite large, including most of the parietal lobe on both sides of the brain. Nevertheless, there are a number of cases of individuals with smaller parietal lesions who have more specific problems. For example, some individuals lose the ability to direct their arm toward visual targets but can nevertheless still make accurate saccadic eye movements toward the same targets. Conversely, there are instances of individuals who can reach out and touch visual targets that they cannot direct their gaze towards. There are also cases of patients who can reach toward an object, but not shape their fingers into the appropriate grasp to pick it up.

We now know that the dorsal stream in humans is located mostly within a long groove known as the intraparietal sulcus (IPS), running roughly horizontally along the upper region of the parietal lobe (see Plate 4, bottom). Functional brain imaging has shown that there are separate areas lying within this sulcus specialized for reaching, saccadic eye movements and grasping, lined up in that order from the back towards the front end. For example, a healthy person can be shown lights in different locations, and asked on each occasion either to turn his gaze to the light, or to reach out to it. When the person has to make reaching movements, the first of these areas (the so-called parietal reach region, or PRR) is activated, whereas when he has to move his eyes rather than his hand—with the very same set of lights serving as targets—the next area in line is activated instead (the lateral intraparietal area, or LIP). If the person is allowed to move both his eyes *and* his hand when pointing to a target (the natural way of doing it) then both areas are activated.

To determine which area becomes specifically activated when a visible target object has to be grasped, it is necessary to 'subtract out' the areas of activation that might result from the eye movements and reaching that usually occur at the same time (see Plate 8 for another example of this subtraction method). This is done by keeping the eyes steady at all times, and by then subtracting the brain's activation pattern for reaching towards objects, point by point, from the pattern obtained during reaching out *and grasping* the same objects. When this is done, only the frontmost of the three areas (the anterior intraparietal area, AIP) shows a net increase in activity. It is worth noting that all of these three areas—for reaches, saccadic eye movements, and grasps—have very close homologues in and around the monkey's intraparietal sulcus, and indeed they were first discovered during single-neuron recording studies in the monkey parietal cortex.

The brains of Ruth and Dee

Characterizing the damage that causes the visuomotor difficulties encountered by patients like Ruth and Anne is relatively easy—they all have clearly defined lesions that can be seen on structural scans such as CT or MRI to include the region in and around the intraparietal sulcus in the upper parts of the parietal lobe. Indeed it was from this fact—documented by Marie-Thérèse Perenin and Alain Vighetto during the 1980s—that it was first possible to infer that the human dorsal stream terminates in the intraparietal sulcus region. More recently these conclusions have been confirmed by the evidence from functional brain imaging already mentioned.

In contrast, Dee's brain damage is less clearly defined, since it resulted from carbon monoxide poisoning, a form of pathology that is rather indiscriminate in its effects. She does not have a complete destruction of the ventral stream, but instead a selective lesion that spares some aspects of ventral stream function, including color perception. In other words, some of the specialized perceptual systems in her temporal lobes appear to be still receiving and interpreting visual messages. Structural MRI scans showed soon after her accident that a large part of her primary visual cortex, V1, was still intact, though surrounded by areas of damage in the neighboring cortical visual areas. More recent MRI scans done at much higher spatial resolution have confirmed this broad picture, but have revealed a particularly dense lesion on both sides of her brain in the ventral stream area most concerned with object perception: area LO. As described more fully in Chapter 8, Dee's lesion corresponds remarkably closely to the extent of LO as mapped on the brains of several healthy volunteers. The LO activations derived from fMRI scans of normal brains have been superimposed onto Dee's structural scan to demonstrate the close correspondence. These striking new findings allow us to offer a much more confident interpretation of her visual form agnosia. In a nutshell, Dee lacks the crucial area that allows us to see that a drawing represents a particular whole object rather than a meaningless fragmented one. Without area LO, we lose our ability to see the structure or 'gestalt' that distinguishes a whole from simply a set of component parts.

As we will see in Chapter 8, fMRI has now allowed us to go further, and gain direct evidence as to what other visual brain areas are still functioning in Dee's brain, and which are not. We will reserve a full discussion of these important new results until Chapter 8. Suffice it to say that these new results provide striking confirmation that areas concerned with the perception of object shape and form in her ventral stream, particularly area LO, are not working properly, whereas the relevant parts of her dorsal stream are.

Exactly why a seemingly generalized form of brain damage, in which the brain is deprived of its oxygen supply, should result in such a selective deficit of form but not color processing subsystems in the ventral stream remains a mystery. It is possible that the distribution of the blood vessels on the surface of the brain (which are never identical in different people) happened to expose Dee's LO more than her other ventral stream areas to the worst effects of the anoxia that did the damage.

Blindsight

Dee has given us some particularly striking and powerful examples of preserved visuomotor control despite profound perceptual disability. Historically speaking, she was the source of inspiration for much of the theorizing that we are summarizing in this book. But she is by no means the first brain-damaged patient in the literature to show 'action without perception'. Some

---

Box 5.2   The asymmetrical brain

One of the unique things about the human brain is its functional asymmetry. It *looks* pretty sym-metrical, just as people do—but like people, it *works* asymmetrically. Most readers will have come across the idea that the left hemisphere is verbal and 'logical', while the right is visual and 'creative'. There is some truth to these notions, though the contrasts are not quite so clear-cut as the popular press would have us believe.

There is good evidence from neuropsychological studies of brain-damaged patients that visual recognition of familiar faces and places is mostly handled by the ventral stream in the right hemisphere. Prosopagnosia and topographical agnosia, for example, arise much more often from right ventral stream lesions than from left. It's the same story in functional brain imaging studies: when people look at pictures of faces and places, there is typically more activ-ation in the face and place areas of their right hemisphere than there is in the corresponding areas on the left. The reason why a good deal of ventral stream processing is concentrated in the right hemisphere is not well-understood. One possible explanation is that many of the corresponding areas in the left hemisphere are busy doing different jobs, particularly those concerned with speech and language. It may be the case that job-sharing between language and visual perception is impossible for any one brain area.

In contrast, the early visual areas are quite symmetrically organized on the two sides of the brain, with the left side of the brain representing the right half of the visual field, and vice versa. In the same way, the motor cortex is symmetrically organized. People with strokes invading the motor cortex in the left hemisphere invariably show a right side motor weak-ness or paralysis, and again vice versa. The fact that the early sensory systems and later motor control systems are completely symmetrical is no surprise. After all, these are the parts of the brain that interact directly with the outside world. They are organized this way in all vert-ebrates. Because the dorsal stream has the job of converting visual input into motor output, it would make sense if it too were symmetrical distributed across both hemispheres. It would not be efficient to have these visuomotor systems concentrated in one hemisphere, since we have to be able to respond to visual targets on our right and left equally well. As it turns out, this is exactly the case. Patients with left or right parietal damage are equally likely to develop optic ataxia. This symmetrical organization of dorsal stream structures is also being confirmed by a growing number of functional brain imaging studies of visuomotor control.

So we have seen why it makes sense for the dorsal stream to be symmetrical. But why is this not the case for the ventral stream? The answer is probably that the ventral stream does not put such a premium on rapid spatially accurate responses in the same way that the dorsal stream does. Its operation in fact is largely off-line—its connections are mostly with semantic and other high-level cognitive systems in the brain, rather than directly with the motor system.

years before we encountered Dee, investigators had discovered a similar and equally striking contrast between visual experience and visuomotor control—but in patients with a rather different kind of brain damage. The lesions in these patients were located in primary visual cortex (V1) on one side of the brain, and consequently left them with an apparently complete blindness in just half of their visual field. The usual way to diagnose this half-blindness (hemianopia) in the clinic is to use a large circular screen or 'perimeter', on which spots of light are flashed at different points while the patient holds his or her gaze steady on a central point on the screen. Hemianopic patients report seeing none of the spots of light that are flashed on the side of the screen opposite their lesion.

As we saw in Chapter 4, the primate perceptual system resides in the ventral stream of visual processing which passes from V1 down onto the underside of the temporal lobes at the sides of the brain. Part of the evidence for this was the research of Charles Gross and his colleagues, who recorded the electrical activity of neurons in this inferior temporal lobe area in monkeys. As we mentioned in Chapter 4, they found that neurons in this region responded selectively to a whole range of different complex visual patterns and objects. Presumably the high-level properties of these neurons are the result of converging inputs from neurons at lower levels of the visual system that respond to the different visual features, such as shape, color and visual texture, that define the objects. Gross and his colleagues went on to show unequivocally that the critical visual input to this form analysis system came from V1. They did this by removing V1 in some monkeys, and showing that the cells in the inferior temporal cortex now remained silent whatever patterns were shown to the eye. So if the human ventral stream is like the monkey's, it will 'see' nothing when V1 is damaged. This would explain why patients with this kind of damage have no visual experience in the affected part of the visual field.

However, Larry Weiskrantz, a neuropsychologist at the University of Oxford, pointed out a strange paradox. Monkeys with damage to V1, who should be just as blind as these hemianopic humans, could detect visual input presented to their 'blind' field. How could this be? One view at the time was that area V1 must have become more important for vision in humans than it was in monkeys. Weiskrantz was reluctant to accept this idea since everything else that was known about the monkey's visual system showed that it was remarkably similar to that of the human. He realized that there was a simpler way to resolve this paradox—one that respected the evolutionary kinship between monkey and human. As Weiskrantz pointed out, monkeys were never asked to *report* on what they saw; instead, they were simply required to choose between two different visual displays or to reach out and grasp a piece of food. In contrast, the human patients were really being asked to comment on their experience: Did they see something out there in the world? All the monkeys cared about was getting their food reward for responding correctly. Weiskrantz suggested that the monkeys with lesions of V1 might be achieving this without having any conscious visual experience at all. They were just guessing—and when they guessed correctly they got rewarded. Perhaps humans, he suggested, could be tested in exactly the same way. In other words, if the patients were not asked 'Did you see the light?' but instead were asked to reach toward it, perhaps they too would show the same spared visual sensitivity as the monkey with V1 lesions.

When patients with V1 lesions began to be tested in this way, a whole panoply of spared visual abilities was uncovered. Patients could point accurately, or move their gaze, toward targets that they insisted they couldn't see. Marie-Thérèse Perenin and Yves Rossetti have more recently found that some patients can even scale their grip and correctly rotate their wrist when reaching out to grasp objects placed in their 'blind' field. Weiskrantz coined the whimsical term 'blindsight' to refer to these various preserved capacities.

So what is going on here? How is it that blindsight patients, and indeed monkeys with V1 lesions, can do these things? After all, the brain damage has closed the front door between the eye and the two cortical visual streams. One clue is that for the most part the preserved abilities are visuomotor in nature. This raises the possibility that more ancient sensorimotor structures, like the superior colliculus, which would still receive visual input from the eyes, could be involved. This would certainly explain how the patients can look toward things they say they cannot see, because the colliculus both receives visual signals directly from the eye and translates those signals directly into eye movements without any help from the cortex.

But this by itself would not account for the fact that blindsight patients can point to or even grasp objects presented in their 'blind' field. These are activities that depend, as we saw earlier, on cortical systems in the dorsal stream. Without a working V1, how could visual information reach the dorsal stream? The answer seems to be that although the ventral stream depends entirely on V1 for its visual inputs, the dorsal stream does not. For example, the French neuroscientist Jean Bullier has shown that neurons within the dorsal stream still respond to visual inputs even when V1 is inactivated by cooling. The most likely route for this information to reach the dorsal stream is again via the superior colliculus, which in addition to its direct role in eye movement control is known to be a way-station along a major visual route from the eyes to the cerebral cortex. This back-door route entirely bypasses V1 and so would remain intact in blindsight patients (see Box 4.1 and Figure 4.2).

In our view, Dee Fletcher's residual vision is ultimately not that different from blindsight. She has the advantage of a largely preserved area V1, through which she retains a much more efficient visual route to dorsal stream areas than the blindsight patient, who has to rely on the more primitive collicular route. Dee is also less severely disabled than the blindsight patient in that only part of her visual experience has been lost—her perception of shape and form. But despite all this, she does resemble the blindsight patient in one important way: that she can perform many motor tasks under visual control while having no perceptual experience of the visual features controlling her behavior.

Summary

We have seen in this chapter that the broad divisions within the visual brain, the ventral and dorsal streams, are themselves subdivided into smaller modules, each with a specific job to do—either a specific kind of visual perception, in the case of the ventral stream, or guiding a specific action, in the case of the dorsal stream. The modularity in the ventral stream presumably reflects the fact that making distinctions within different perceptual categories requires that different kinds of information be extracted from the incoming visual signals. The modularity in the dorsal stream, however, is dictated by the need to convert visual information into different kinds of actions. In the next chapter, we will examine how the different demands of visual perception and the visual guidance of action have determined the ways in which the visual information is handled in the two streams.

6

Why do we need two systems?

The evidence seems pretty clear that we humans have two visual systems: one for perception and one for the visual control of action. We suggested in Chapter 4 that this division of labor must have emerged in our primate ancestors because of the different processing demands imposed by these two functions of vision. But what are these different demands of perception and action, and how are they reflected in the way the two streams deal with the visual input? What does conscious perception need to know that the visual control of action does not—and vice versa?

First let us revisit for a moment what natural selection has 'designed' the two systems to do. Visual perception is there to let us make sense of the outside world and to create representations of it in a form that can be filed away for future reference. In contrast, the control of a motor act—from picking up a morsel of food to throwing a spear at a fleeing antelope—requires accurate information about the actual size, location and motion of the target object. This information has to be coded in the absolute metrics of the real world. In other words, it has to be coded in terms of the actual distance and size of the objects. In addition the information has to be available at the very time the action has to be made.

These two broad objectives, as we shall argue in this chapter, impose such conflicting requirements on the brain that to deal with them within a single unitary visual system would present a computational nightmare.

A TV-watching module in the brain?

Perception puts objects in their context. We perceive the size, location, and motion of an object almost entirely in relation to other objects and surfaces in the scene. In other words, the metrics of perception are relative, not absolute—a fact that explains why we have no difficulty watching television, a medium in which there are no absolute metrics at all (Figure 6.1). Actually, the fact that we can follow what is happening on television is quite remarkable. All that we really see, after all, is patterns of light, shade, and color that are constantly shifting and changing over a small two-dimensional surface in front of us. Yet we have no trouble segregating these patterns into meaningful objects and making sense of the complex events the images represent.

The only metrical information that is available on TV is based on the relations between objects that are depicted on the screen, and our previous knowledge of their real geometry. Sometimes,

Figure 6.1

Whether or not a person, a building, or even Godzilla is represented by a small image on a TV screen or a large image on a movie screen is irrelevant to our understanding of what is going on. In fact, sometimes a person might fill the whole screen and sometimes be only a tiny figure running away from Godzilla. What matters to our perception is the *relative* size of people and things on the screen. But while we have no difficulty perceiving what is happening on the screen, we cannot reach out and grasp the things that are represented there. This is because the images do not the reflect the real size and position of objects in the world in relation to us. Watching television convincingly mimics our experience of the world. What it cannot mimic is the visual information that we need to act on the world.

for example, a face might fill the entire screen; on other occasions, it might be one of a sea of faces in a crowd. Yet in both cases we know that it is a face and we also know that it is closer in one case than the other. Worse still, there are unpredictable changes in the point of view. Here we are at the mercy of the camera operator, the editor, and the producer of the program—and yet, even with the fast jump-cuts and scene transitions that typify music videos and advertising, we have little trouble figuring out what is going on. The size, shape and distance of objects can be inferred only from our knowledge of real world geometry, from the relations among different objects in the scene, and from assumptions about continuity from one scene to the next. Despite all this, even young children have an immediate and natural understanding of what is unfolding on a TV screen.

Understanding television is not, of course, what our visual system evolved to do. We do not have a special 'TV-watching module' in our brains. And yet television tells us something important about perception. Television simply would not have developed as a major medium for communication if our visual brain were not somehow receptive to the way in which it represents the world. There is little doubt that the brain mechanisms that allow us to watch and understand TV are the very same mechanisms that allow us to perceive and understand the real world. In real life too, the brain uses stored knowledge of everyday objects, such as their size, to make inferences about the sizes of other objects and about their distance from us and from each other. In order to extract the meaning and significance of the scene before us, we only need the relative size, position, and speed of the objects with respect to one another. We do not need to know the absolute metrics of every object in the scene in order to make sense of the visual world.

In contrast, this kind of relative information is of little help in the control of action. To pick up a coffee cup, it is not enough to know that it is further away than the bowl of cornflakes and closer than the jar of marmalade; and knowing that the whole scene represents a breakfast table doesn't help much either. The brain systems that program and control our grasping movements must have access to accurate metrical information about the location of the cup and its real size. Furthermore, information about the cup's location and real distance must be computed in egocentric frames of reference—in other words, in relation to the observer rather than in relation to other objects.

Television can provide us with all kinds of useful general knowledge about the world around us, but it would be a hopeless medium for *acting* on things in the world. We might recognize a can of beer on a commercial but we could never pick it up—not just because it isn't real but because we see the beer can from the changing points of view of the camera operator and not from our own (see Figure 6.1). It is true that video images can be used successfully in a number of applications where humans are controlling robots or other instruments and a direct view of the workspace is not available. In these cases, however, the point of view and the magnification of the image are kept relatively constant. Imagine the disaster that would occur if a surgeon had to carry out a video-assisted operation in which the camera was moved around at the same speed and unpredictability as in a music video!

These arguments about the different requirements of perception and visually guided action lead to two important conclusions. First, since the computations leading to action must be metrically accurate (and highly reliable), they must depend on visual mechanisms that at some stage are quite separate from those mediating our perception of the world. Second, because different kinds of actions (e.g. manual grasping movements versus saccadic eye movements) require that the computations be performed within different egocentric frames of reference, there are likely to be several different visual mechanisms for the control of action, each specialized for the control of a different effector system. As we have seen in the preceding chapters, nature seems to concur; that is, natural selection has created in primates a brain that embodies these design principles. To put it another way, the different computational demands of perception and action have presumably been a major driving force in the evolution of the visual brain.

Time and the observer

Humans, like most other animals, rarely stay still for more than a few seconds at a time, except perhaps when they are sleeping. Indeed even when seated at our desk, we move our eyes around, swivel in our chair, and lean back and stretch occasionally. In other words, we rarely stay in a static relationship with objects that we may need to interact with. Yet we have no difficulty in reaching out and answering the phone, picking up our coffee cup, or shaking a colleague's hand when he or she comes into the room. We do all of these things, even though the patterns falling on the retinas of our eyes are constantly changing. Of course we 'know', at one level, where the coffee cup is—it's on our desk, to the right of the telephone. But if we want to pick up the cup, our brain needs to compute exactly where the cup is with respect to our hand. Moreover the brain has to come up with that information just as we are about to move. Relying on a computation made even 5 seconds earlier would be useless, except in the unlikely event that we (including our eyes) have remained completely immobile for that length of time. In other words the only way we can successfully and reliably guide a movement towards a goal object at a particular moment is by having continually updated visual information available to us. This means that the brain has to compute the precise parameters needed to specify an action immediately before the movements are to be initiated. By the same token it would make little sense to store this information for more than a fraction of a second, whether or not the action is actually performed. Not only would its value be strictly time-limited, it would be positively disadvantageous to keep the information hanging around in the system.

Of course it cannot be denied that we are well able to make reaching and grasping movements using 'old' visual information,

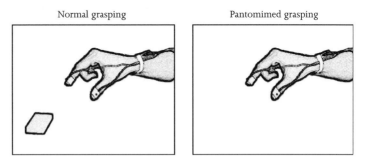

| Normal grasping | Pantomimed grasping |

Figure 6.2
In normal grasping, we reach out and pick up the object we see in front of us. In 'pantomimed' grasping, we see the object but then it is taken away. After a few seconds' delay, we then reach out and pretend to pick it up. Grasping an object that we can see engages the automatic visuomotor systems in the dorsal stream, whereas pantomimed grasping requires that we use a conscious visual memory of what we saw earlier—a memory that was constructed by the ventral stream.

even after an object has been taken away—for example we can pretend to grasp a cup of coffee that was located in a particular spot on our desk, even minutes later. In one sense these actions are visually guided, even though the visual information is no longer present. But these movements are quite different from the smooth and well-calibrated movements we make under direct visual control. This has been studied in the laboratory by having people look at a solid rectangular block (the Efron blocks described in Chapter 2) and then wait for several seconds in the dark before initiating a grasping movement. During the delay, the object is removed, and the person is asked to 'pantomime' how they *would* have picked it up (see Figure 6.2). These pantomimed movements are slower, less accurate, and somewhat stylized: not surprisingly, given that the person is showing you *how* to do something rather than actually doing it. This change in the character of the movement is present even after a delay as short as 2 seconds. Of course the person will still open the hand grip more widely for larger than for smaller objects, just as when making real grasps, though they generally do so later in the movement. These pantomimed grasps also tend to be smaller than real grasps—probably because people do not realize that the hand opens much wider than the width of target object during real grasping movements (see Figure 2.3).

In contrast to the unrealistic efforts that most of us can make, mime artists can produce very convincing movements to imaginary objects—and indeed convey a whole story by doing so. They can almost convince us that they are climbing a ladder, washing a window, picking up a heavy object, or peeling a banana, just by making movements in mid-air. They do this by first studying closely how such movements are actually made—and exaggerating certain aspects and not others. But the important thing is that while it takes no special skill to pick up a real teacup, it requires the well-practised skill of a mime artist to perform that very same action convincingly when the teacup is imaginary. Moreover, unlike the mime artist, we pick real things up without thinking about the details of the object or the movement. It is only when we have to perform an action off-line that we have any difficulty.

When students in a lab experiment pretend to pick up a block after a 2-second delay, they are undoubtedly using a similar strategy to that of the mime artist, but without the mime artist's practised eye for detail. They are presumably bringing to mind the visual appearance of the object they are pretending to grasp, though in this case after only a short delay since seeing it. Of course the person first has to have perceived the object, so as to have the information to hold in memory in the first place. But as we have argued throughout this book, such perceptual processing is not at all what we use to program and control a normal on-line grasping movement. It is only in the artificial case of pretending to grasp an object that we need to rely on stored information derived from our perception of that object. So what would happen if a person had no perception of the object's shape and dimensions in the first place? Would that mean that they could not perform the pantomime grasping task at all?

The reader will remember that our agnosic patient Dee Fletcher, who cannot perceive the form and dimensions of objects, still shows excellent scaling of her grasp when she reaches out to pick up objects in real time. To do this, she must be relying entirely on her visuomotor system, since she has no access to relevant perceptual information about the objects. Yet despite this excellent on-line ability, if our argument is correct, Dee should have great difficulty when asked to perform pantomimed grasping of those same blocks. Now, of course, she could no longer rely on her visuomotor system—its visual information would have decayed before she could use it. But nor could she use her perceptual system as a healthy person would, since that is profoundly disabled. Dee would not be able to recall the dimensions of the block she was shown 2 seconds earlier, because she wouldn't have had a perceptual experience of those dimensions in the first place.

Dee behaves just as these arguments would predict. Her attempts to pantomime the act of picking up the different blocks show little or no relationship to their actual size. Evidently, Dee has no perceptually coded information about the block she just saw that could serve to guide her movements—even though only 2 seconds have elapsed between last seeing the block and initiating her grasp. It is not that she cannot pretend to grasp the blocks. She goes through the motions, but her attempts bear little resemblance to the actual dimensions of the object shown to her. In fact as we mentioned in Chapter 2, she has no problem making pantomimed actions that do not depend on what she has just seen, but which are based instead on memories of objects already familiar to her. If asked to imagine an everyday thing like a grape-fruit or a hazelnut, she can reach out and pretend to pick it up, opening up her grip entirely appropriately as she does so—large for the grapefruit and small for the hazelnut.

The same difficulty that Dee has in scaling her grasp to objects she has just seen also shows up in her ability to point to a flashed target light a few seconds after it has been switched off. In exactly the same way, her accuracy when pointing to a such a small target is as good as a normal person's when she is allowed to point while the target is still on. But when she has to wait for a few seconds she makes much bigger errors than other people do.

In other words, then, Dee has a rather general problem in dealing with visual information when she is not allowed to use it imme-diately it is given to her. When there is no delay, it seems that she can use her visuomotor system as efficiently as anyone else. It is only when the task requires the use of memory for previously perceived events that her performance falls apart. As we have already argued, since Dee's perception of the location and geom-etry of objects is compromised, she has no information to store in memory and as a consequence no information on which to base a pantomimed action.

But what about patients who have the opposite pattern of brain damage to Dee's, in other words patients with dorsal stream dam-age? What would they do in the pantomime task? Such patients are unable to use vision effectively to control their actions in the here and now: in other words, they have optic ataxia. We would make the paradoxical prediction, however, that their performance should improve if they were forced to refrain from responding to the visual target, and instead to make a pantomimed movement a few seconds later. After all, their perception of the world is rela-tively spared, so that during the imposed delay they would be able to invoke their perceptual memory of the target to help them plan their response. In other words, they should do better after a delay than they would if they responded to the target immediately. This prediction has been borne out in tests of both delayed pointing and delayed pantomime grasping.

In collaboration with Marc Jeannerod and his colleague François Michel, we tested Anne Thiérry, the patient we introduced in Chapter 3 who had developed optic ataxia following damage to both of her parietal lobes. The defining symptom of optic ataxia, of course, is that the patient is unable to make accurate reaching movements toward a visual target. Anne is no exception to this. When we tested her ability to point to briefly flashed spots of light she made big errors, often ending up several centimeters away from the target. But remarkably she made much smaller errors when asked to delay for 5 seconds after the light spot had gone off before making her pointing attempts. This really is a surprising result, because healthy subjects *never* get better when asked to point after a delay—in fact they get worse. (As we mentioned earlier, Dee gets much worse.)

It is very difficult to explain Anne's improvement, except by assuming that she is able to use a quite different system—one that is still relatively intact—to perform the delay task. This spared system, we argue, is her perceptual system, which is not designed to guide immediate responses but does become useful when the response has to be pantomimed. When Anne responds in real time, her faulty visuomotor system leads inevitably to errors in performance. When she has to wait, however, her preserved perceptual system can be used just as it is in healthy people performing the same task, and so she does much better. In other words, despite Anne's extensive brain damage, her relatively intact perceptual system can still permit a visual memory of the light's location to be stored. This visual memory can presumably then guide her successful pantomimed responses.

More recently, along with Yves Rossetti and Chris Dijkerman, we have tested a younger woman, Irene Guitton, who like Anne, suffers from optic ataxia following damage to both parietal lobes, but who has little sign of other aspects of the Bálint syndrome. Irene's pointing improved when she was forced to delay doing it, just like Anne's. Not only that: she also improved her grasping as well. In other words, she scaled her grip better when pantomiming than when simply grasping an object placed in front of her—the exact opposite of Dee Fletcher. These complementary results provide a convincing package. They mean that Irene shows a direct double dissociation with Dee between immediate and delayed grasping—she gets better after a delay, while Dee gets much worse.

All these experiments on delayed responding make the point that the dorsal (action) stream works in real time and stores the required visuomotor coordinates only for a very brief period—at most for a few hundred milliseconds. The modus operandi appears to be 'use it, or lose it.' The ventral (perception) stream, on the other hand, is designed to operate over a much longer time scale. For example, when we meet someone, we can remember his or her face (though not always his or her name) for days, months and even years. This difference in time scale is a reflection of the different jobs the two streams are designed to do. But the difference in time scale is not the only distinction between the dorsal and ventral streams. As discussed at the beginning of this chapter, the two streams actually 'see' the world in different ways, using quite different frames of reference.

Scene-based versus egocentric frames of reference

When we perceive the size, location, orientation and geometry of an object, we implicitly do so in relation to other objects in the scene we are looking at. In contrast, when we reach out to grab that same object, our brain needs to focus on the object itself and its relationship to us—most particularly, to our hand—without taking account of the visual context, that is, the scene in which the object is embedded. To put it a different way, perception uses a scene-based frame of reference while the visual control of action uses egocentric frames of reference.

A scene-based frame of reference makes sense for perception because it allows the brain to use all kinds of information to identify objects and their relationships, and then to piece together the meaning of the scene. The job of perception, after all, is to construct a useful internal model or representation of the real world outside. This representation can then serve as a visual foundation for our mental life, allowing us to make inferences about objects in the world and their causal relations, and to decide between different courses of action based on this knowledge.

The use of scene-based metrics means that the brain can construct this representation in great detail without having to compute the absolute size, distance and geometry of each object in the scene. To have to take in the absolute metrics of the entire scene would in fact be computationally impossible, given the rapidity with which the pattern of light changes on our retina. It is far more economical to compute just the relational metrics of the scene, and even these computations do not generally need to be precise. It is this reliance on scene-based frames of reference that lets us watch the same scene unfold on a small television or on a gigantic movie screen without being confused by the differences in scale.

Whenever we look at something in the world, we cannot help being influenced by the scene that surrounds it. We are obliged to see some things as closer or further away than others, and some things as smaller or larger. The contrast in size between objects is a constantly familiar experience in our perceptual life. For example, when we see an average-size person standing next to a professional basketball player, that person suddenly appears far smaller than they really are. Of course when we get more information by seeing more of the scene, then the true sizes of the two become clearer. Size contrast is perceptual in nature and not a trick of optics. It depends on assumptions that our brain makes about the sizes of objects. For example, our brain, on the basis of previous experience, 'knows' that houses are always bigger than people. Film versions of *Gulliver's Travels* make use of this by filming the same actor against artificially small- or large-scale backgrounds. Even though we know it is the same actor, we cannot help but see him as a giant in one case and as a miniature human in the other.

But as we noted earlier, scene-based metrics are the very opposite of what you need when you act upon the world. It is not enough to know that an object you wish to pick up is bigger or closer than a neighboring object. To program your reach and scale your grasp, your brain needs to compute the size and distance of the object in relation to your hand. It needs to use absolute metrics set within an egocentric frame of reference. It would be a nuisance, and potentially disastrous, if the illusions of size or distance that are a normal part of perception were to intrude into the visual control of your movements.

If there really is a difference between the frames of reference used by perception and action systems, it should be possible to demonstrate this in the laboratory. The advent of virtual reality displays, where the experimenter has exquisite control over the way in which objects are presented to the observers, has made this kind of experiment a practical possibility (see Figure 6.3). Artificial 'objects' of different sizes can be created and shown to the observer without the possibility of familiarity with particular real objects obscuring the interpretation of the experimental results. In addition it is a simple matter to control the precise period for which the virtual object is visible on the screen.

Figure 6.3

The Virtual Workbench. The observer sees the image of what is on the computer monitor by looking at a mirror while wearing special glasses that make the image three-dimensional. The object depicted on the computer monitor appears to be located below the mirror. When the person reaches out to grasp this virtual object, his hand encounters a real object whose position coincides exactly with what he sees. The computer and robot arm controlling the position of the real object are linked so that every time the virtual object is placed at a new location the real one moves accordingly.
From Hu, Y. & Goodale, M.A. (2000). Grasping after a delay shifts size-scaling from absolute to relative metrics. *Journal of Cognitive Neuroscience*, 12, 856–868 (Figure 2).

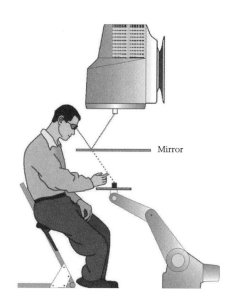

Mirror

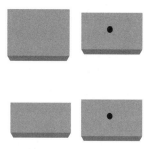

Figure 6.4

When you look at a block (marked with a dot) accompanied by a larger block, it looks slightly smaller than when you see it accompanied by a smaller one. When you reach out to grasp the block, however, your hand opens in-flight to match the real size of the target block irrespective of the size of its companion. In short, perception is affected by the contrast in size, but the visual control of action is not.

Using this technique, we showed undergraduate volunteers a series of three-dimensional virtual images of target blocks, each of which was paired with an image of another block that was always either 10 per cent wider or 10 per cent narrower than the target block. The blocks were never visible for more than half a second. The target blocks were marked with a red spot. Just as in our previous studies with brain-damaged patients, each student was asked to do one of two things. The student either had to reach out and grasp the target block using the index finger and thumb or to indicate manually the size of the block, again using the finger and thumb. To ensure a natural grasp, the display was designed so that there was a real but unseen block in the same location as the virtual target.

The reason for having two objects, a companion block as well as the target block, was to induce a 'size-contrast effect' (see Figure 6.4). It was anticipated that the observer's perception of the target's size would be unavoidably influenced by the presence of a larger or smaller companion. This is exactly what happened. The students consistently judged a target block paired with a large companion as smaller than the same target when it was paired with a small companion. In contrast, when they reached out to *grasp* the target object, they opened their hand to an identical degree whichever companion it was paired with. In other words, the scaling of grip size to the size of the target block was not at all subject to the size-contrast effect that was so compelling during perceptual judgments.

This result is an instructive one. It confirms that the scene-based coding of size that is such a ubiquitous feature of our perceptual experience does not apply at all to the visual coding of size that is used to guide the action of grasping. Of course, it makes good sense to have a visuomotor system that works with real size rather than relative size, so it shouldn't be so surprising that the system is immune to the size-contrast effect. Nonetheless, we can see here a graphic example of our actions being controlled by visual information that is clearly different from our conscious visual experience.

The calibration of grasp does fall victim to the size-contrast illusion, however, when a delay is inserted between viewing the objects and initiating the grasp movement. When the student subjects had to wait for five seconds before picking up the target object that they had just seen, the scaling of their grasp now fell prey to the influence of the companion block. Just as they did when they made perceptual judgments, they opened their hand wider when the target block had been accompanied by a small block than when it had been accompanied by a large block. This intrusion of the size-contrast effect into grip scaling *after a delay* is exactly what we had predicted. Since the dedicated visuomotor systems in the dorsal stream operate only in real time, the introduction of a delay excludes their use. Therefore when a delay is introduced, the calibration of the grasp has to depend on a memory derived from perceptual processing in the ventral stream, and becomes subject to the same size-contrast illusions that perception is prone to.

These size-contrast results dovetail nicely with the observations we made of pantomime grasping made after a delay in our visual agnosic and optic ataxic patients. Dee Fletcher couldn't do the delayed task at all, while Anne and Irene's performance actually improved. Dee could do only the immediate task (using her relatively intact dorsal stream), while Anne and Irene could do the delayed task better (using their relatively intact ventral stream).

Visual illusions

The size-contrast effect we have just discussed is an everyday occurrence—you do not need to arrange things in any special or artificial way to see it. But there are many other ways in which our eyes can be fooled. The perceptual illusions that result will often be far larger, though they generally require a more carefully contrived scenario. No undergraduate course on visual perception would be complete without a session devoted to these illusions. We never fail to be impressed with the fact that our eyes can deceive us so thoroughly—and even when the trick is explained we continue to perceive apparent differences in size, orientation, movement, and distance that we know are not really there. Many visual scientists would agree with British psychologist Richard Gregory, who has argued over many years that illusions are not just curiosities, but can provide important insights into how the brain constructs our percepts of the world.

One major class of illusions depends on so-called pictorial cues—the kinds of cues that are commonly exploited by painters to create a realistic three-dimensional world on a two-dimensional canvas (see Box 6.1). The artist's manipulation of cues like perspective and relative size can create powerful illusions of depth and scale, taking advantage of the way in which our brains carry out an obligatory analysis of the visual scene that confronts us. Such cues are one of the most important sources of information used by the perceptual system to construct our representations of the world. One particular example illustrates this well. The central circles in the top two arrays shown in Figure 6.5 are actually identical in size—but it is very hard to resist the impression that the one on the left (surrounded by small circles) is larger than the one on the right (surrounded by larger circles). We can neutralize the illusion by increasing the size of the central circle surrounded by larger circles, as shown in the lower part of Figure 6.5. In this case, although the two central circles look alike, they are actually quite different in size.

A number of explanations have been put forward to account for this illusion, which was first described by the late nineteenth-century German psychologist Hermann Ebbinghaus. The most commonly accepted one goes something like this: The brain cannot help but 'assume' that the array of smaller circles represents a cluster of objects more distant than the array of larger circles. To use a term we will enlarge on later in this chapter, the perceptual system is attempting to maintain 'size constancy' across the entire visual array. This remains true even though each cluster includes an object (the central circle) that is different in size from the majority. So the central circle within the array of smaller circles will be perceived as more distant than the central circle within the array of larger circles. Since the two central circles are actually identical in size as far as the

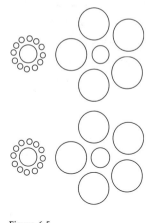

Figure 6.5

In the Ebbinghaus illusion, shown here, the two middle circles in the top two arrays appear to be different in size even though they are actually physically identical. The two middle circles in the bottom display appear to be identical but their real size is actually different. (To convince yourself of this, view each display through a piece of paper with two holes cut in it that reveal only the two central circles.)

Left: When this cheap flashlight was placed on the table in front of Dee, she said: 'it's made of aluminium. It's got red plastic on it. Is it some sort of kitchen utensil?' She guessed it was something for the kitchen—probably because a lot of kitchen implements are made of metal and plastic. As soon as the flashlight was placed in her hand, Dee knew exactly what it was. 'Oh. It's an electric torch!' she said. See Chapter 1, p. 8 for more details.

Right: The edges of objects can be defined in a number of different ways—by differences in luminance (a boundary between light and dark regions), differences in color, differences in visual texture, or differences in the direction of motion. In everyday life, the edges or boundaries of objects are typically determined by combinations of these different cues. Thus, when we see a dark green van driving down a snowy road, differences in luminance, color, visual texture, and motion all contribute to our perception of the van. See Chapter 1, p. 10 for more details.

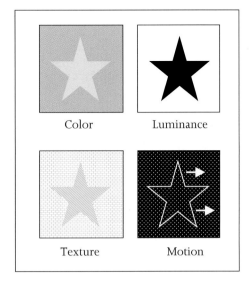

Left: Dee cannot identify line drawings of objects. Not surprisingly, therefore, she cannot recognize the line drawing of the flower shown here. Nor does she do much better with a black and white photograph. Dee can recognize objects depicted in color photographs, however—particularly if the color and other surface features are 'diagnostic' of the object. When presented with the color photograph shown here, for example, she said 'Oh! It's a flower. I think it's an African violet.' She doesn't use the color-defined edges to see the shape of an object; instead she appears to use color to identify its material properties. In other words, she sees the textures and colors of the leaves and petals of the African violet without seeing its overall shape. See Chapter 1, p. 8 for more details.

Plate 1

Left: Detail from *Slave Market with the Disappearing Bust of Voltaire.* Salvador Dali was an expert at devising paintings in which more than one image is depicted. Top-down knowledge about the shapes of faces causes one to see the bust of Voltaire, in which the facial features are actually made up of two figures dressed in black and white clothing. Alternatively, one can choose to see the figures rather than Voltaire.

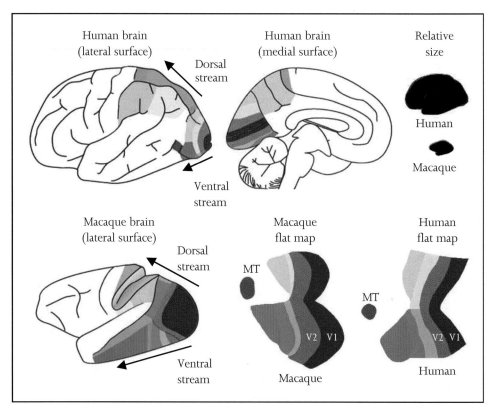

Above: Monkey and human visual areas. The colored regions indicate the location of visual areas in the macaque monkey and human cerebral cortex. Note that more than half of the cortex in the monkey is devoted to some kind of visual processing. In the human brain, the visual areas are located much more posteriorly and medially. When the cortex is artificially flattened, the similarity in the layout of the early visual areas in the two species can be readily seen. In these flat maps, only the areas that have a 'map' of the retina or are sensitive to motion (MT) are shown. Higher-order areas are omitted. For more details see Chapter 4, p. 48. (Adapted from Hadjikhani, N., Liu, A.K., Dale, A.M., Cavanagh, P., & Tootell, R.B.H. (1998). Retinotopy and color sensitivity in human visual cortex. *Nature Neuroscience,* 1, 235–241.)

Plate 2

Left: This painting, entitled *Vertumnus*, is one of a series by Italian painter, Giuseppe Arcimboldo (1527–1593), that depicts faces constructed of other objects, in this case fruits and vegetables. When the object agnosia patient, Charles K., looked at this painting, he saw the face right away but failed to identify any of the fruits and vegetables that make up the face. See Chapter 5, p. 59 for more information. Reproduced here with permission from The Art Archive/Skoklosters Slot Balsta/The Art Archive, Ref: AA348075. Desc: Emperor RUDOLF II 1552–1612 as Vertumnus c.1591. Artist: ARCIMBOLDO, Giuseppe:1527–93:Italian.

Below: This painting by the American artist, Bev Dolittle, *The Forest has eyes*, conceals a number of faces hidden in the trees and rocks. Whereas the face in the Arcimboldo painting is immediately obvious, the faces here are much more difficult to see. But Charles K. spotted them immediately—and was not confused by the other elements of the painting, which to the normal observer are far more salient. See Chapter 5 for more information. (Permission sought.)

Plate 3

Right: Areas in the ventral stream that are involved in the visual recognition of places, faces, and objects. These areas are marked on a mathematical three-dimensional reconstruction made from an anatomical MRI scan of a young man's brain, viewed here from below. (Note that the face area is typically much larger in the right hemisphere.) The depiction of the cortical surfaces shown here offers a more faithful representation of what the brain really looks like in 3D. The images of the brain shown below, however, give a better impression of the brain's topography. See Chapter 5, pp. 60–63 for more details about the functions of the different areas shown on the right.

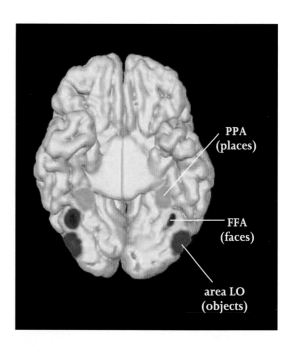

PPA
(places)

FFA
(faces)

area LO
(objects)

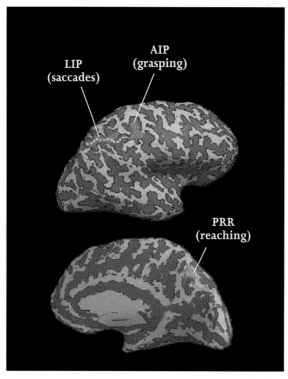

LIP
(saccades)

AIP
(grasping)

PRR
(reaching)

Left: Areas in the dorsal stream that are involved in the visual control of the eyes, arm, and hand are shown on this fMRI map which has been superimposed on an 'inflated' brain (one in which the regions that are normally buried in the fissures have been exposed by mathematically inflating the brain rather like one might blow up a crumpled paper bag). The hills or gyri have been colored light blue; the valleys or sulci have been colored gray. The visuomotor areas are clustered along a fissure in the posterior parietal cortex called the intraparietal sulcus or IPS (shown with a broken line in the top picture). See Chapter 5, p. 65 for more details about the functions of these areas.

Plate 4

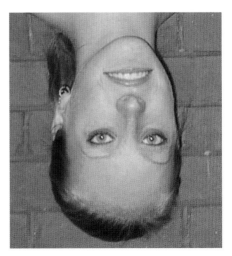

Above: These two photographs of a young woman illustrate the specialized nature of face processing, in which the normal upright face is treated as a whole rather than as a collection of separate features. If you turn the page upside down, your face processing module will immediately allow you to see that there is something dreadfully wrong with one of the pictures! When viewing the page the right way up, the face on the right looks relatively normal because upside down faces do not engage the 'holistic' face processing module and instead the brain has to deal with each feature separately. For more details, see Chapter 5.

Above: Carefully examine the two pictures here and the corresponding pictures on the next page. Can you spot the differences? Pairs of picture like these which have a difference in one quite major feature have been used to demonstrate 'change blindness'. When viewing such pictures successively, observers often fail to notice the difference, particularly in pictures like the one showing the two children. The more perceptually salient difference in the picture of the young woman is easier to see, even though it is less physically salient than the difference in the picture of the children. For more details, see Chapter 6.

Plate 5

Above: The drawing on the left, which was drawn at age 6, shows the typical absence of pictorial cues to distance and size in young children's drawings. There is no perspective, no occlusion, and no size scaling with distance. There is however relative size scaling (the table is larger than the people) and distance is signalled by the height of objects in the picture (the people at the top are further away). The drawing on the right, which was done a year later, begins to incorporate some additional pictorial cues including occlusion and size scaling with distance. For more details, see Chapter 6. (Reprinted with the kind permission of Ross Milner.)

Above: See previous Plate.

Plate 6

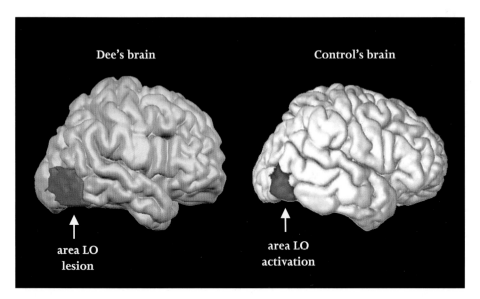

Above: Area LO, a ventral-stream area implicated in object recognition, is damaged on both sides of Dee's brain. For comparison, area LO has been localized on the brain of a healthy control subject by comparing fMRI activation to intact versus scrambled line drawings. See Chapter 8, p. 122.

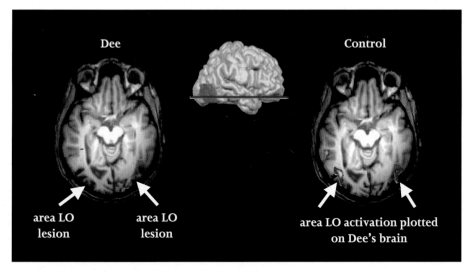

Above: These MRI images were taken through Dee's brain at the level marked with a red line on the whole brain. Unlike the control subject, Dee showed no difference in fMRI activation with intact as compared to scrambled line drawings. The robust activation seen in the control subject on the same task has been mathematically transformed so that it could be plotted on Dee's MRI scan. The location of this activation coincides closely with the lesions on both sides. For more details, see Chapter 8, p. 122. (From James, T.W., Culham, J., Humphrey, G.K., Milner, D.A., & Goodale, M.A. (in press). Ventral occipital lesions impair object recognition but not object-directed grasping: An fMRI study. Brain.)

Plate 7

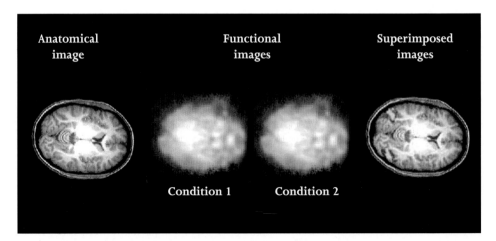

Anatomical image	Functional images	Superimposed images

Condition 1   Condition 2

Above: The subtraction logic frequently used in functional neuro-imaging research. Scans of the activity patterns in the brain in the experimental condition (say viewing intact line drawings of objects—'condition 1') are compared with scans derived from a control condition (say viewing fragmented versions of the same drawings—'condition 2'). The difference (shown on the right) represents the areas specifically activated by object drawings, 'subtracting out' more basic visual processing. Conventionally 'false colors' are used in producing these difference maps, showing the 'hottest' areas in yellow, the less hot in red, and so on. These colored areas are superimposed on an anatomical MRI image of the brain of the same individual. All of the scans shown here represent a horizontal cross-section through the brain at the level of the temporal lobe. See Box 5.1 and Chapters 5 and 8.

Right: The 'grasparatus' devised by Jody Culham. The subject lies in the dark inside the MRI magnet. The solid shapes appear in front of the subject as the cylinder is made to rotate stepwise by a pneumatic motor. The target shape is presented by turning on a bright LED behind the shape. The task is either to grasp the target shape, or in a control condition, to simply touch it with the knuckles. As the difference map on the far right shows, a cross-section through Dee's parietal lobe reveals selective activation in an anterior part of the intraparietal sulcus (area AIP) when she grasps the target object. This activation is similar to that seen in control subjects. See Chapter 8 for more details. (From Culham, J.C., Danckert, S.L., DeSouza, J.F.X., Gati, J.S., Menon, R.S., & Goodale, M.A. (in press). Visually-guided grasping produces activation in dorsal but not ventral stream brain areas. Experimental Brain Research.)

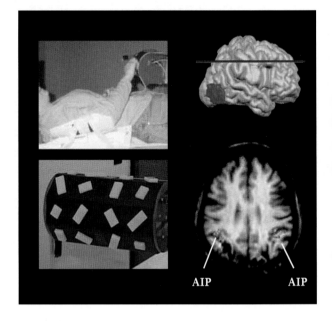

AIP   AIP

Plate 8

Box 6.1   Pictorial cues to depth and scale

For centuries, painters have exploited cues that our perceptual system uses every day to understand the world. For example, in the real world, objects that occlude our view of other objects
in the scene must be closer to us than the occluded objects. In this famous engraving by
Albrecht Dürer (1471–1528), the table occludes part of St Jerome and thus is seen as nearer.
More distant objects in general are located higher in our visual field than nearby ones. Thus
the lion, which is located lower down in the scene is perceived as being closer. Familiar size
is also useful. Our knowledge of the real size of lions and people gives a strong indication of
their relative position in the scene depicted in this engraving. Moreover, our knowledge of
these familiar objects gives information about the size of other less familiar objects that are
nearby. Geometric perspective, of course, is a particularly powerful and frequently used cue
to distance—and this cue is exploited to good effect in Dürer's engraving. The tricks that artists
use to convey depth and scale in pictures are as powerful as they are because they reflect the
processes we rely on all the time to perceive the real world.

retina is concerned, the perceptual system 'infers' that the central
circle that appears to be further away must be the larger of the two.

Mechanisms such as these, in which the relations between
objects in the visual array play a crucial role, are clearly central to
the operation of perception. In fact, the perceptual system appears
to be unable to avoid making comparisons between different

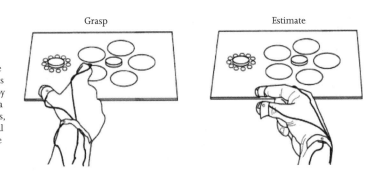

Grasp   Estimate

Figure 6.6

A three-dimensional version of the Ebbinghaus illusion. In this experiment, subjects were asked either to reach out and grasp one of the disks, or simply to show us what they thought the size was by opening their finger and thumb a matching amount. On some trials, the disks were physically identical whereas on other trials they were perceptually identical. From Haffenden, A. & Goodale, M.A. (1998). The effect of pictorial illusion on prehension and perception. *Journal of Cognitive Neuroscience*, 10(1), 122–136 (Figure 3).

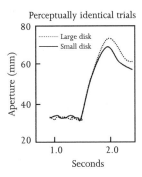

Figure 6.7

A graph showing the changing distance between the finger and thumb (grip aperture) as a typical subject reaches out to pick up two disks, one of which is physically larger than the other. Even though the subject believed that the two disks were the same size, their visuomotor system was not fooled by the illusion. In other words, they scaled their grip aperture to the real size of the objects. From Aglioti, S., DeSouza, J., & Goodale, M.A. (1995). Size-contrast illusions deceive the eyes but not the hand. *Current Biology*, 5(6), 679–685 (Figure 4).

elements in a scene. As a consequence, the perceptual system is vulnerable to the kinds of illusory displays devised by Ebbinghaus and many others. Even though you know full well that you are looking at an illusion, you cannot resist it: your beliefs are over-ruled by your perception. These distortions have little practical significance for our perception of the world—their rare occur-rences are far outweighed by the usefulness of the scene-based systems that cause them. Of course as soon as you *act* on the world, such distortions could lead to problems. Imagine the prob-lems that could occur if some accidental conjunction of objects in the visual field created an illusion of size or distance that not only fooled your perception but also your visuomotor control. But as we have already seen, the visuomotor system is largely isolated from perception. Its *modus operandi* seems to be to disregard information from much of the scene when guiding goal-directed movements like grasping, restricting itself to the critical visual information that is required for that movement. To test this idea, we devised, in collaboration with Salvatore Aglioti, a new version of the Ebbinghaus illusion. We used solid disks, rather like poker chips, as the target circles, and displayed them against the classic Ebbinghaus background. The set-up is illustrated in Figure 6.6.

Now we could not only test people's perception of the sizes of the disks, but we could also see whether or not the scaling of their grasp was affected by the illusion. As it turned out, although people showed robust perceptual illusions—even in a matching task in which they opened their index finger and thumb to match the perceived diameter of one of the disks—their grip aperture com-pletely resisted the illusion and was instead tailored to the real size of the disk when they reached out to pick it up (see Figure 6.7). Since we first carried out this experiment some years ago, several

88

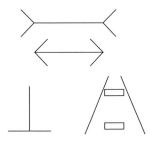

Figure 6.8
Three other pictorial illusions that have been found to have little effect on the visuomotor system. The well-known Müller–Lyer illusion is shown at the top. The two lines between the arrowheads appear to be different lengths. In the horizontal–vertical illusion (bottom left) the vertical line appears to be longer than the horizontal. In the Ponzo (or railway-lines) illusion, the upper bar appears to be longer than the lower bar. In all of these illusions, the pairs of lines (or bars) are actually identical in length. When these lines are replaced by solid rods or bars and subjects asked to pick them up end to end, although the illusion is still present perceptually, it has little effect on the in-flight scaling of their grasp.

other perceptual illusions have been adapted to test the their effects on visually guided action (see Figure 6.8). In nearly all cases, the illusions have been found to have little or no effect on the scaling of grasp or the trajectory of a reaching movement despite having strong effects on perception.

The exceptions that have been found are themselves interesting. For example, when a delay is introduced between viewing the Müller–Lyer illusion and initiating a reaching movement directed at one end of the illusion line, suddenly the illusion begins to affect movements to a quite dramatic degree. But of course, this is exactly what we would expect on the basis of our discussion earlier in this chapter. Visuomotor control works in real time. When a delay is imposed, perception intrudes. And if perception is influenced by an illusion so is the delayed movement.

In other cases, a visual illusion may affect visuomotor control because it acts at an early stage of visual processing, before the visual system splits into its two cortical streams. In collaboration with Richard Dyde, we used two different illusions of orientation (see Figure 6.9). We found that the patterns shown in the bottom of the figure elicit just as strong an illusion when the observer 'posts' a card toward the central grating as when he or she adjusts the card at a separate place to match the apparent tilt of the target. Yet when a rod or grating is set within a large frame (as shown on the top of Figure 6.9), although perception is affected equally powerfully, no illusion at all is apparent when a grasping or posting action is made toward it. These results fit nicely with the generally accepted views of how the two illusions work. The first illusion is believed to be generated within the primary visual cortex, so that its effects would be passed on to mislead both visual streams in the brain. But by all accounts the second illusion is a context- or scene-based one, and would therefore be expected to come into play within the ventral stream alone.

How does the dorsal stream compute size and distance?

If the visuomotor system is not using pictorial cues to compute the size and distance of goal objects, what information is it using? Presumably whatever cues are used, they would have to be reliable and accurate—and certainly not subject to illusion. In other

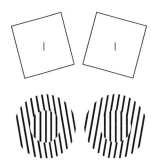

Figure 6.9
The 'rod and frame illusion' (top) and the 'simultaneous tilt illusion' (bottom). In both illusions we see the central line or stripes to be tilted in opposite directions according the tilt of the frame (top) or striped background (bottom). The reasons for this, however, are different for the two illusions. The rod and frame illusion depends on the same kinds of perceptual mechanisms as the pictorial illusions already mentioned, and like those affects perception but not action. The simultaneous tilt illusion, however, is probably the result of local effects within the primary visual cortex, and therefore would be passed on to both visual streams. As a consequence this illusion affects both perception and action.

Figure 6.10
When we fix our gaze on an object in the middle distance (b), then that object falls on the same point on our two retinas. However objects in front of or behind that will fall on non-corresponding points, allowing the brain to compute their distance from the viewer relative to the point of fixation. This powerful cue to depth is called stereopsis. In addition the extent to which the two eyes are converged on the fixated object gives a measure of its absolute distance from the observer. These two binocular cues to distance (stereopsis and convergence) complement the various pictorial cues discussed earlier.

words, they would have to be independent of the visual context within which the goal object is seen. One way of computing an object's distance (and, as we shall see, its size) takes advantage of the fact that we have two eyes. Because the two eyes each have a different view of the world (technically known as stereopsis) and our brain has information about their degree of convergence (i.e. the slight difference between their lines of sight), it is possible to compute the real distance of an object we are looking at (see Figure 6.10). Moreover, because the image of the object will have a certain size on the retina, the brain can use this distance information to compute the object's actual size, effectively using simple trigonometry. This kind of computation is highly reliable and will deliver accurate size and distance information independent of the details of any particular scene.

Of course we are all familiar with the power of binocular cues to depth through watching 3D films and looking through 'Viewmaster' stereoscopic viewers. But although these artificial contrivances give strong, even exaggerated, perceptions of depth, the pictorial cues that are already present even in a single eye's

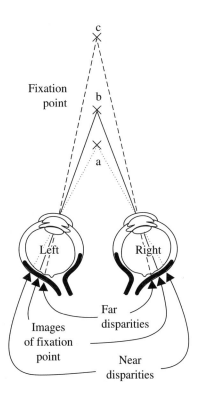

view of the scene are powerfully compelling for perception. For example, when we see a painting by one of the old masters, we are highly influenced by the pictorial cues like perspective that are emphasized in the picture, even though we not only know that the picture is flat, but we also have binocular information from our two eyes telling us that it is flat (see Box 6.1). Exactly the same argument can be made for TV and the movies, in which the images contain no binocular depth information. (As with the paintings, we ignore the binocular depth information that tells us that the screen is in fact flat.) Even when we look at the real world, binocular information makes only a small contribution to our *perception* of depth. The simple act of covering one eye will reveal that this is true. While there is some reduction in the richness of the percept, the world still looks remarkably three-dimensional.

Where binocular vision really comes into its own is when we have to act on the world—particularly on objects within arm's reach. Try threading a needle with one eye closed! Experiments that have tested people's reaching and grasping under monocular viewing conditions have shown that the reaches are much slower, more tentative and less accurate than the same movements made under normal binocular viewing conditions. It is binocular information (derived from stereopsis and/or monitoring of the convergence angle of the eyes as we look at the goal object) that allows us to make grasping movements that are calibrated correctly for distance and tailored to the real size of the object.

Presumably then, it is binocular vision that allows the visuo-motor system to escape the effects of pictorial illusions like the Ebbinghaus. It simply doesn't use, and isn't affected by, the pictorial cues that the illusion exploits. But if the visuomotor system instead relies heavily on binocular cues, then how does it locate objects when one eye is covered? There are other cues, like the motion of the world on our retina when we move, that the system can and does use. In fact, patients who have lost an eye through accident or disease move their heads a lot when picking up objects to compensate for the loss of binocular vision. But we can also use pictorial cues when we have to. If you cover one eye and keep your head stationary, you can still pick up objects, though not quite as well as you normally do. In this case, you must be relying almost entirely on the pictorial cues provided by your perceptual system, which explains why you are not doing quite so well. Pictorial cues simply do not provide the accurate metrics that the visuomotor system requires. Interestingly, when people are tested on the visuomotor version of the Ebbinghaus display with only one eye open, the scaling of their grasping movements now becomes sensitive to the illusion.

Dee Fletcher, of course, because of her visual form agnosia, does not have access to most pictorial cues. Her visuomotor system has to rely almost entirely upon its normally preferred source of depth information; in other words, on binocular vision. Without binocular vision, her visuomotor system is lost. When Dee was tested on a grasping task with one eye covered, her grip scaling became surprisingly inaccurate. In fact, she opened her hand wider for a given-size object the closer that object was to her. Without the help of binocular cues, she could not compute the real size of the object as a normal person would because she could not correct for viewing distance. Without binocular information, she couldn't tell if a given image on her eye represented a large object far away or a small object close up.

What information does the dorsal stream derive from binocular viewing? It could be stereopsis, in that Dee's brain might directly compute viewing distance from a comparison of the different views that each eye receives. But alternatively, it might be that she simply fixates her gaze on the object, and then somehow monitors how much her eyes are converging on it. In fact, this turns out to be what she does. With Mark Mon-Williams and Rob McIntosh, we found that her reaches under binocular conditions when she pointed to targets set at different distances is critically dependent on how much she converges her eyes when looking at the target. We discovered this by artificially making her eyes converge too much or too little, using a wedge prism placed over one of her eyes. She made big errors in the extent of her reaches that could be almost entirely accounted for by the geometry of the prism. In other words, her brain must have been relying very heavily on monitoring her eye convergence in computing how far to reach. Normal observers too are affected by such prisms, but not to anything like the extent to which Dee is affected. They of course have access to pictorial cues like perspective, which they can use to help them gauge distance—the same cues that imbue paintings with their apparent depth. But because these cues depend on form perception, they are unavailable to Dee.

How does the ventral stream construct our visual world?

At the beginning of this chapter, we suggested that the perceptual system uses scene-based coding and relational metrics to construct a rich and detailed representation of the real world. The ultimate reason for having such representations is so that we can use them as a foundation for thinking about past, present and future visual worlds and for planning our actions. To serve such a generalized function, our memory bank of information about objects in the world has to be in a form that is independent of the particular viewpoint from which the objects were first encountered. That is, the perceptual system has to abstract the invariant aspects of objects, which can then serve, as it were, as *symbols* for what we see in the world. The system has to distance itself from the details of each individual view of the object on the retina. It has to get away from the fact that the projected image of a door on the retina could be rectangular or trapezoidal, according to the viewpoint from which we see it. That instantaneous view may be important for grasping an object, but it is a distraction when what we wish to store is the identity of the object. What we perceive is a door.

Primitive art and the drawings of young children, paradoxically, reflect the high-level abstract nature of our perceptual representations. In some sense, children are representing what they 'know' rather than what they 'see'. When young children draw a busy scene, all of the objects in the scene—people, cars, houses, and so on—will be in full view (see Plate 6, top). No object will obscure part of another; nor will objects be scaled for viewing distance. Nor do their drawings incorporate perspective to take into account the observer's viewpoint. For an artist to render a 'faithful' representation of a scene takes years of training and considerable mental effort. The artist has to *deduce* the perspective projection of a scene on the eye; it is not a direct perceptual experience. For example, returning to the door for a moment, we may see a wide open door or one that is closed—but what we are not aware of is a narrow trapezoid in one case and a wide rectangle in the other. To draw the open or closed door, we have to 'work backwards' to reconstruct what instantaneous snapshot would create that perception. In other words, we have to put on the canvas what the light from the scene has put on our retina.

This aspect of perception, in which different projected image shapes are interpreted as being the same object, is called shape constancy. This is one of a number of so-called constancies, which collectively ensure that we recognize a given object pretty much independently of the particular viewing conditions. Other constancies include color constancy, brightness constancy, and size constancy. So for example, a blue shirt looks blue both indoors under fluorescent lighting or outdoors in bright sunlight—even though the wavelengths of light hitting the retina under the two conditions are very different. Similarly, a black T-shirt outdoors on a sunny day certainly looks black even though it actually reflects more light into the eye than does a white T-shirt seen indoors. And two identical balls, one viewed close by on a beach and another seen 30 meters away are both perceived as the same size, despite one occupying much more area on the retina than the other. All of these constancy phenomena cooperate to help us interpret the many objects that we may see in a complex scene, and there is a continuous 'bootstrapping' process, in which each object provides part of the context for the others.

The boundary between perception and knowledge is not a sharp one. Not only does perception inform knowledge, but also knowledge constantly informs perception. We have all experienced perceptual learning. The novice, whether he is a beginner at microscopy, bird watching, or military surveillance, will literally not see things in the same way as the expert. This use of knowledge to shape our perceptual experience (what we called top-down processing in Chapter 1) is a principle used in many machine recognition systems, such as those designed for recognizing hand-written script. In a real sense, what we 'see' in our perceptual experience is determined in good part by what we already know.

The influence of previous knowledge on perception has led some theorists to argue that what we experience is a representation of a virtual, not a real, world. What they mean by this is that our knowledge of the world helps us construct a rich and complex experience that is derived as much from memory as it is from visual input. The influence of memory and expectation can be seen in the familiar children's game in which you have to spot the difference between two almost identical pictures. Experimenters like Ron Rensink and Kevin O'Regan have taken this game to new heights. Using modern computer graphics, they have doctored photographs of everyday scenes to generate pairs of pictures that are identical except for one feature. When they show these pairs of pictures on a computer screen one after the other, it takes most people many alternations to spot the difference. In fact some people never do see the difference, until it is pointed out to them. Take a look at the two pictures of young children shown in Plates 5 and 6. Even though the difference between them, once spotted, is obvious, you probably didn't see it immediately. In fact, to find the difference, you may have had to resort to the strategy of carrying out a point-by-point comparison. And if you hadn't been told to look for a difference, you would probably never have seen it. Both pictures convey the same meaning—and the difference between them is not essential to that meaning. In fact, the difference in physical terms can be quite large—but as long as that difference is not central to the meaning of the scene, it will not be noticed. On the other hand you probably spotted the difference between the two pictures of a young woman also shown in Plates 5 and 6 far more quickly. Although the difference is small, it changes our whole percept of the face, and faces are generally the prime targets of our attention, even when a scene contains many other elements.

Film-making again provides wonderful examples of how our expectations determine a good deal of what we see. What is apparently a continuous piece of action is often in fact a pastiche of scenes taken at different times that have been strung together. The order in which the scenes were actually filmed is often quite different from how they unfold on the screen. It is the job of the continuity editor to make sure that the scenes fit together seamlessly and that, for example, an actor with a moustache at the beginning of a scene is still wearing it at the end. Fortunately for them, they do not have to do this perfectly. They can make big mistakes and still get away with it—particularly when the mistakes they make are not crucial to the narrative. In other words, even if the picture on the wall is present in one scene and missing in the next, most people in the audience will not notice.

Perception, then, is not a passive process, in which we simply experience whatever is on our retina at any one time. It is also more than just a simple matching of incoming information and stored templates that have been built up from previous visual experiences. Instead, it seems that much of what we 'see' is an internal invention based on plausible assumptions about what is out there in the world. We do not validate these assumptions until we actually look directly at things in our visual environment—yet subjectively we have the impression of a stable and complete world that extends throughout our visual field, rich in detail and meaning. But just as a film set made of painted plywood façades, with the occasional cardboard cactus, may suffice in a Western movie—and is a great deal cheaper to use than filming on location—it seems that we unwittingly make do with ersatz visual experience much of the time in real life as well. It's only when we focus our attention on a part of the visual field that our experience becomes fully informed about what's actually out there in the world.

Summary

Visual processing in perception and action are very different. They differ in their time constants: very short for action, indefinitely long for perception. The two systems differ also in their metrics: one is object-based and relational, the other is viewpoint-dependent and uses real-world metrics. And one system is knowledge based and top-down, while the other works from the optic array using first principles, in a bottom-up way. So how do these two totally different systems manage to work together in harmony?

7

Getting it all together

Throughout this book, we have been advancing the idea that the ventral perception stream and the dorsal action stream are two independent visual systems within the primate brain. Nevertheless, the two evolved together and play complementary roles in the control of behavior. In some ways, the limitations of one system are the strengths of the other. The ventral stream delivers a rich and detailed representation of the world, but throws away the detailed metrics of the scene with respect to the observer. In contrast, the dorsal stream delivers accurate metrical information about an object in the required egocentric coordinates for action, but these computations are fleeting and are for the most part limited to the particular goal object that has been selected. Of course somehow the two streams must end up cooperating harmoniously with each other, and the fact that they do so doesn't mean that the distinction between them thereby disappears. After all, to invoke a metaphor used by our colleague Yves Rossetti, a husband and wife may have utterly different personalities, habits and ways of thinking; but that doesn't mean they cannot live a successful and closely cooperative life together.

The close interplay between the two streams is something that can be seen in almost everything we do. For example, suppose while walking down the street, you recognize an old friend walking towards you, someone that you have not seen for a long time. As the friend draws near, you reach out and shake his outstretched hand. This familiar experience illustrates the different but complementary roles played by the two visual streams in our everyday social behavior. It is your ventral stream, through its intimate connections with long-term memory, that enables you to recognize your friend—and to see the significance of his outstretched hand. But it is your dorsal stream that enables you to grasp his hand successfully.

Although it might seem inefficient and even cumbersome to have two specialized visual systems, which then have to be coordinated, this arrangement has some important advantages over a single 'jack-of-all-trades' system.

Putting thought into action

As it turns out, a useful way of understanding the need for two systems, each doing a different job, can be found in robotic engineering. In fact, a close analogy to the relationship between the two visual streams is provided by *tele-assistance* (see Figure 7.1). Tele-assistance is one of the general schemes that have been devised whereby human operators can control robots working in hostile environments, such as in the crater of a volcano or on the surface of another planet. In tele-assistance, a human operator identifies and 'flags' the goal object, such as an interesting rock on the surface of Mars, and then uses a symbolic language to communicate with a semi-autonomous robot that actually picks up the rock.

A robot working with tele-assistance is much more flexible than a completely autonomous robot. In some environments, of course, flexibility is not so important. Autonomous robots work well in situations such as an automobile assembly line, where the

Figure 7.1

In tele-assistance, a human operator looks at a distant scene displayed on a video monitor. The video signal is provided by a camera mounted on a robot at the scene. If the operator notices an object of interest in the scene, she flags that object so that the robot can then locate it and retrieve it for later analysis. The operator needs to know little about the real distance and scale of the object; the robot can figure that out by itself using on-board optical sensors and range finders. By the same token, the robot needs to know nothing about the significance or meaning of the object it is retrieving. In our model of the visual system, the ventral stream plays a role analogous to that of the human operator, whereas the dorsal stream acts more like the robot.

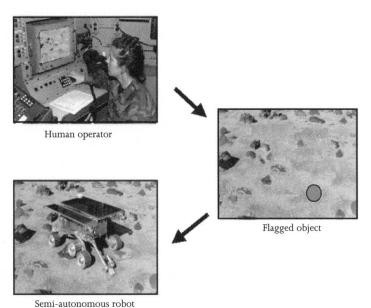

Human operator

Flagged object

Semi-autonomous robot

tasks they have to perform are highly constrained and well specified. These tasks can be quite complex and precise, depending on detailed sensory feedback from the actions performed. But autonomous robots can accomplish such highly precise operations only in the working environment for which they have been designed. They could not cope with events that its programmers had not anticipated. Imagine the difficulty, for example, of programming an autonomous robot so that it could deal with everything it might encounter on the surface of Mars. Clearly there is no way of anticipating all the possible objects and variations in terrain that it might confront. As a consequence, it might fail to react appropriately to critically important objects or events that it encounters. It would be oblivious to things that the scientists were not looking for in the first place, yet which might have been of great importance to investigate.

At present, the only way to make sure that the robot does the right thing in unforeseen circumstances is to have a human operator somewhere in the loop. One way to do this is to have the movements or instructions of the human operator (the master) simply reproduced in a one-to-one fashion by the robot (the slave). For instance an operator in a nuclear plant might move a joystick that directly controls the movements of a robot arm in a radioactive laboratory. But such tele-operation, as this method of control is sometimes called, cannot cope well with sudden changes in scale (on the video monitor) or with a significant delay between the communicated action and feedback from that action. This is where tele-assistance comes into its own.

In tele-assistance the human operator doesn't have to worry about the real metrics of the workspace or the timing of the movements made by the robot; instead, the human operator has the job of identifying a goal and specifying an action toward that goal in general terms. Once this information is communicated to the semi-autonomous robot, the robot can use its on-board range finders and other sensing devices to work out the required movements for achieving the specified goal. In short, tele-assistance combines the flexibility of tele-operation with the precision of autonomous robotic control.

Our current conception of how the two visual streams interact in the animal or human brain corresponds nicely to this engineering principle. The perceptual systems in the ventral stream, along with their associated memory and other cognitive systems in the brain, are rather like the human operator in tele-assistance. They identify different objects in the scene, using a representational system that is rich and detailed but not metrically precise. When a particular goal object has been flagged, dedicated visuomotor networks in the dorsal stream, in conjunction with output systems elsewhere in the brain (located in other brain structures including the premotor cortex, basal ganglia, and brainstem) are activated to perform the desired motor act. In other words, dorsal stream networks, with their precise egocentric coding of the location, size, orientation and shape of the goal object, are like the robotic component of tele-assistance. Both systems have to work together in the production of purposive behavior—one system to select the goal object from the visual array, the other to carry out the required metrical computations for the goal-directed action.

Of course in drawing this analogy with tele-assistance, we do not wish to underestimate the future possible developments in the design of autonomous robots. Clearly engineers are making great strides on this front. One day it is quite likely that the role of the human operator could be incorporated into the design of the machine. But how would you set about building such a super-robot? What kind of visual system should it have? The lessons learned from biology tell us that there would be little prospect of success in trying to give such a robot a general-purpose visual system, one that both recognizes objects in the world and guides the robot's movements. As we have argued throughout the book, the computational demands of object recognition and scene analysis are simply incompatible with the computational demands of visuomotor control. A much more effective design for the super-robot would be to emulate the division of labor between the ventral and dorsal visual streams in the primate brain.

There would need to be an intelligent processing module in the robot, one that can analyze scenes and select appropriate goals on the basis of both current input and information stored in its knowledge base (both built-in and learned). The most efficient way for this module to operate would be to construct a representation of the world based on relational metrics computed within a contextual or world-based frame of reference. But these computations, while crucially important for determining goals, would not be directly helpful in guiding the robot's actual movements in achieving those goals. To do this would require a separate set of dedicated and metrically precise sensorimotor modules, ones that are specialized for carrying out the just-in-time computations that determine the parameters of the specific actions required to achieve the specified goal. Only when such a super-robot is designed and built would the human operator become redundant. Then the robot could be truly said to be putting its thoughts into action.

In robotic tele-assistance, the human operator can communicate with the semi-autonomous robot via radio. The operator can flag the intended target by indicating its position on the videomonitor at the control center. That position is not the location of the target in the real world of Mars but rather simply its position on the screen, which corresponds precisely to the robot's-eye-view. The robot now has all the information it needs to zero in on the object. The operator can then select the appropriate motor command from the robot's repertoire, such as 'retrieve', and the robot does the rest. But what happens in a biological tele-assistance system like that found in the human brain? How does the ventral stream tell the dorsal stream what the target is and what to do with it?

Certainly there is good evidence from brain anatomy that the two streams are interconnected. But just how the ventral stream flags the location of the intended target in a coordinate system that the dorsal stream can understand is not immediately obvious. After all, as we discussed in the last chapter, the ventral stream works in scene-based coordinates and is more attuned to where an object is relative to other things in the world than where it is relative to the observer. But to control actions such as grasping, the dorsal stream has to know where an object is, not with respect to other objects, but rather with respect to the hand. And if it is going to control another kind of action such as kicking a ball, it has to know where the ball is with respect to the foot. So the two systems are using entirely different frames of reference—speaking a different language in fact—and yet somehow the ventral stream has to tell the dorsal stream which object to act upon.

One way that this could happen is by taking advantage of the fact that the information feeding in to both systems comes from the same source—the retina and early visual areas such as primary visual cortex. These low-level visual processors contain a two-dimensional 'snapshot' of whatever the eyes are looking at. Although this information is passed on separately to the two streams where it is used for different purposes, the pathways are actually two-way streets. In other words, there are lots of back-projections from higher-order areas in both streams back down to primary visual cortex. In fact it is now well established that the back-projections frequently outnumber the forward-going ones. This means that the two streams could communicate indirectly with one another via these back-projections to the shared origins of their incoming signals. Since these early signals are still coded in retinotopic coordinates, it would be possible for the ventral stream to flag a target for the dorsal stream using this common frame of reference. Once a target has been highlighted on the retinal map, it can be converted into any other coordinate system that the dorsal stream might need to use.

Imagine that a target for a grasping movement had been highlighted by the ventral stream in this way. Since the dorsal stream now knows where the target is on the retinal map, it might compute the target's location with respect to the hand in the following way. First the dorsal stream computes the position of the eye with respect to the head, then the position of the head with respect to the body, and finally the position of the hand with respect to the body. It can now work out where the target is with respect to the hand. Similar kinds of computations could be used to compute where a soccer ball is located with respect to the foot. In other words, once the dorsal stream gets a fix on the retinal location of a goal object, it can transform that information in whatever way it needs to control a huge range of different actions. Although the dorsal and ventral streams have their own sophisticated and specialized languages, they both still retain contact with the more basic language of the retina. Rather like the human operator can instruct the robot via the two-dimensional optical array behind the lens of the robot's camera, so the ventral stream can instruct the dorsal stream via the common retinotopic map in early visual areas.

Recent research implicates another likely player in this scenario—LIP—an area in the dorsal stream that plays an important role in the voluntary control of eye movements (see Plate 4, bottom and Chapter 5). This area also seems to be critical for shifting our attention from one object to another in a visual scene, even when we don't move our eyes. In other words, the control of attention may have 'piggy-backed' (in evolutionary terms) on the control of eye movements. Current fMRI evidence suggests that LIP somehow transmits its current attentional 'searchlight' to the ventral stream, perhaps again via downstream projections back to early visual areas, such as primary visual cortex. In fact, there is evidence from neurophysiological studies that when a monkey pays attention to a particular location, the activity of neurons corresponding to that location in primary visual cortex is enhanced. It appears that there is constant two-way traffic between the streams, and that the most likely route for this is via early visual areas.

All of this is highly speculative and over-simplified. We do not know for sure how the two streams communicate. But research on interactions between the two streams is well underway in visuo-motor laboratories around the world, and holds the promise of explaining in detail how 'seeing' and 'doing' work together. The final answers to these questions will probably owe as much to detailed analyses of behavior as to neurobiological investigations.

Top-down control of action

In drawing the analogy with tele-assistance, we do not wish to imply that the ventral stream plays only a very distant role in the implementation of action, rather like a chief executive officer in a corporation, setting goals and writing mission statements and then delegating the real work to others. In many aspects of behavior, the ventral stream plays a much more hands-on role than this.

The ventral stream contributes directly to certain aspects of motor programming, notably those that depend on information that cannot be derived in a bottom-up manner, directly from the retina. If you think about it for a moment, most of the time, when you pick up an object, your fingers typically close around it with just enough force so that it will not slip out of your fingers when you lift it, but not so much force that you damage it. In other words, the force you apply has to be scaled appropriately for the object's weight (and its other characteristics) from the moment your fingers make contact, well before any feedback from touch and other somatosensory receptors comes into play. Unlike the size, location, orientation, or even shape of an object, which can be computed from the projected image on the retina, the object's mass, compliance (how hard or soft the object is) and surface friction can be gleaned only through experience.

Take the case of two objects of roughly the same size but different weights: say a phone book and a box of crackers. You will automatically apply more grip force when you pick up the phone book than when you pick up the box of crackers. Of course, you already have a good idea about how heavy phone books and boxes of crackers are. But you can only make use of this knowledge to calibrate your grip force if you recognize the object in the first place. Such recognition, as we have seen, has to be carried out by visual mechanisms in the ventral, not the dorsal, stream.

But there is another twist to the story. When you pick up unfamiliar objects that are made of the same material but are not the same size, you typically apply more grip force to the larger object than you do to the smaller one—presumably because your brain makes the entirely reasonable assumption that the large object weighs more than the small one. At first sight, this might look like the kind of thing the dorsal stream could do. After all, it already computes object size for scaling the opening of the hand in flight as it approaches the object. Why couldn't the dorsal stream simply use the information it already has about object size to scale grip force when you pick up the object? But this apparently straightforward task is beyond the capabilities of the dorsal stream alone, because more information than size is needed. The force you need to apply is determined not so much by the size of the object, as its weight. This means that the brain has to know about the properties of the material that the object is made of. Just like the phone book example, the brain has to use its stored visual knowledge about the density of different materials. For example, you would apply much greater force to pick up a large stone than you would to pick up a piece of polystyrene of the same size (unless of course the polystyrene had been painted to look like a stone, as it might be on a film set—then you might get a surprise!).

This computation of grip force, then, is a joint product of visual size and stored knowledge about the density of the material from which the goal object is made. The dorsal stream, which we know is dominated almost entirely by its current visual input, could never by itself compute the weight of an object. Of course, it is possible that the dorsal stream still computes the size of the object, even though it is the ventral stream that is needed to figure out what the object is made of. But it is also possible that the ventral stream does both jobs. After all, it does compute size all the time in constructing our perceptual experience. So we are confronted with the question: Which stream computes size for grip force? One way to answer it is to see whether or not pictorial illusions, which are known to affect the perception of size but not the scaling of grip size, affect the scaling of grip force. If the dorsal stream controls the force as well as the size of the grip, then grip force should not be affected by the illusion. If the ventral stream provides the size information, however, then grip force, like perception, should be affected by the illusion.

Stephen Jackson, a psychologist at the University of Nottingham, has carried out this very experiment. Instead of using the Ebbinghaus Illusion which we described in Chapter 6, Jackson used the Ponzo or railway-lines illusion, in which an object placed within the converging end of the two lines looks larger than one placed within the diverging end (see Figure 6.8). As expected, when people reached out to pick up an object placed in these two different positions, their grip aperture was scaled to the real, not the perceived size of the object. What surprised Jackson, however, was that their grip force *was* affected by the illusion. In other words, his participants scaled their grip force to the perceived, not the real size of the object, applying more force when the object looked (deceptively) bigger. So the answer to the question about how we compute grip force is clear: the whole job appears to have been left in the hands of the ventral stream. Consistent with this, we have found that Dee Fletcher has real problems with adjusting her grip force when objects of different size are used—that is, when she has only *visual* information about their size. When she can also *feel* the object's size, she adjusts her grip appropriately.

The semantics of action

When you pick up a knife, you usually pick it up by the handle, not the blade. When you pick up a screwdriver you do the same thing even though, unlike the knife, there is no danger of cutting yourself. In other words, many objects, especially tools, elicit 'use-appropriate' postures. Even when the screwdriver is positioned with its handle pointing away from you, you will typically turn your hand right around in a slightly awkward fashion and grasp it by the handle as if you were about to use it (see Figure 7.2). It

Figure 7.2

When we pick up a screwdriver, even when we are not going to use it, we typically grab it by the handle. In the picture on the left, the person picks up the screwdriver by the handle despite the fact that he has to adopt an awkward hand posture to do so. When he is pre-occupied with a memory task, however, he will often pick up the screwdriver using a grasp which is well-shaped but unrelated to tool use (as shown in the picture on the right). Dee, who cannot recognize screwdrivers and other tools, shows a similar tendency to pick them up efficiently but inappropriately when the handle is facing away.

goes further than that. Your intentions come into the equation as well. Say you are going to put the knife into the dishwasher. If you intend to make sure that the blade of the knife is pointing upwards in the rack, then you will probably grab it by the blade (carefully) when you take it off the table. In short, the function of an object and what you intend to do with it will dictate how you pick it up.

But when you are faced with an object, how does the brain know what the appropriate way to grasp it is? First and foremost, the brain has to know what the object is. This is clearly a job for the ventral stream. But an important part of recognizing an object, particularly a manufactured object, is knowing what it is for. This means there must be links between the ventral stream and our stored information about how the hand should grip the object in order to use it. The use of these functional semantics in selecting the appropriate grasp has been shown in an elegant experiment carried out by Sarah Creem and Dennis Proffitt at the University of Virginia. They presented undergraduate volunteers with a series of tools and implements, such as a toothbrush, a frying pan, and a screwdriver, with the handles turned away from them. Needless to say, when the students reached out to pick up these objects, they still grabbed the handle even though this meant adopting an uncomfortable posture. If, however, they were doing this while they simultaneously tried to recall words they had learned before, they picked up the object as if blind to its functional semantics. Nonetheless, although they grasped the objects inappropriately, they still picked them up deftly, showing well-calibrated grasps. In other words, the dorsal stream was still doing its job as well as ever—it was just the functional aspects that were missing. They were missing presumably because the word-memory task was putting heavy demands on the high-level cognitive processes needed to retrieve the functional semantics of the object and thus the appropriate grasp to use. Indeed, Creem and Proffitt showed in another experiment that tasks which did not have a large semantic component but which nevertheless demanded the students' attention did not interfere with the functional aspects of their grasps.

These results strongly suggest that it is the ventral rather than the dorsal stream that provides us with visual information about the function of an object. If this is so, then we would expect that someone whose ventral stream is damaged, such as Dee Fletcher, would pick up everyday objects rather like the students did when they were engrossed in the word-memory task. In other words, she should make 'grasp mistakes' when asked to pick up manufactured objects such as a knife or a screwdriver that are oriented with the handle pointing away. In fact, Dee does show mistakes of this kind. When she reaches out to pick up such objects (ones she cannot identify by sight), her grasp is perfectly matched to the object's size, shape, and orientation, but shows no indication that she understands its function. Thus, she grasps the screwdriver by its shaft rather than its handle—and only then rotates it in her hand so that she can hold it properly. In other words, because her damaged ventral stream is unable to process the screwdriver's shape, Dee has no idea what it is ahead of time and is therefore unable to select the appropriate part of the object to grasp. Nevertheless, the intact visuomotor systems in her dorsal stream can still compute the required metrics to ensure that her grasping movement, however inappropriate, is well formed and efficient.

So is the ventral stream a visuomotor system as well?

Well, not exactly. But ultimately everything the brain does is done in the service of action. Otherwise brains would never have evolved at all. As we pointed out in Chapter 4, natural selection operates on the consequences of action, not on the consequences of thought alone. The ventral stream makes contributions to action in several ways. For example, it is the ventral stream that identifies the goals for action, and that enables the brain to select the class of action to perform. The ventral stream, as we have seen, also plays the dominant role in deciding how much force to apply when picking things up, and probably also how hard we kick a soccer ball.

In practice it is going to be very difficult to tease apart the different elements that are contributed by the two streams even in an apparently simple everyday action like picking up a coffee cup. For example it is your ventral stream that allows you to identify the objects on the table and to distinguish your cup from others that might be there. It is your ventral stream, too, that allows you to single out the handle from the rest of the cup, so that you can then select the appropriate hand posture for picking up the cup to take a drink of coffee. But having identified the handle of your cup and the action you wish to perform, it is then up to the visuo-motor machinery in the dorsal stream to get your hand and fingers positioned efficiently on the cup's handle. In addition to this, the scaling of the initial forces that you apply to lift the cup to your mouth is based on the stored information about the weight of the cup, which you have to access through your ventral stream. So although your dorsal stream takes the responsibility for transforming the visual metrics of the goal into a smooth and efficient movement, your ventral stream does not remain aloof and uninvolved. It is closely involved in the action at all levels, not just at the planning stage but right down to the programming of the force you apply with your fingers.

Conscious and unconscious vision

We began the book by introducing Dee Fletcher, a young woman who has lost all visual experience of the shapes of objects. We have often asked Dee what the world looks like to her. She finds it very hard to put it into words. As we mentioned earlier, she sometimes says that things 'run into each other' so that she finds it hard to tell where one object ends and the other begins, especially when the two objects have a similar color or are made from the same material. She also mentions that things often look 'fuzzy' to her. But, as we noted, it is not like the experience that a short-sighted person has when he takes off his glasses. Don't forget that Dee has excellent acuity—she can see fine detail. The problem may be that we are asking Dee to talk about what she doesn't see—we are asking her to describe what is *not* there in her conscious experience. The same questions have been asked of patients with blindsight. These people have a complete absence of visual experience in the visual field opposite their brain damage. But they don't say that everything on that side looks blank or that there's some kind of hole in their field of vision. They find the question impossible to answer. Just as you would find it impossible to say what you 'see' beyond the edges of your visual field, or behind your back. So perhaps we are expecting too much of Dee when we ask her what she sees. She cannot describe what she cannot see.

Yet despite the fact that Dee has no conscious visual experience of object shape, she retains the ability to use information about the shape to guide her actions. Dee's case, along with evidence from a broad range of studies from frogs to humans, tells us that visual perception and the visual control of action depend on quite different brain systems. What we have learned from these studies is that conscious visual experience of the world is a product of the ventral not the dorsal stream. You might perceive the tennis ball that has just been lobbed over the net by your opponent, but you can never be conscious of the particular information that your visuomotor system uses to guide your successful return. This visuomotor computation happens entirely unconsciously. You are not aware of the fact that the ball is expanding at a certain rate on your retina and that this is an important cue for knowing exactly when to swing to hit it with the 'sweet spot' of the racquet. When you are running around the court chasing the ball, the visual scene is changing on your retina quite dramatically. The shape of the projected image of the net, for example, will be constantly changing—and yet you will continue to see the net as a stable and unchanging object in the scene. It is perhaps a good thing that you are not aware of all of these viewer-dependent changes. If you were, the world would become a bewildering kaleidoscope of unrelated and disconnected experiences in which objects change their sizes and shapes as you move about. What you need are the enduring constancies of perception in order to make sense of the world.

But how does the ventral stream *give* us that elusive mental quality of 'awareness'? This raises the general question: how can physical states in *any* part of the brain give rise to conscious states? These questions present philosophical and empirical problems that are currently impossible to solve. Nonetheless, the first experimental steps in approaching these questions have already been taken. These first steps skirt around the philosophical minefields by only asking what *correlations* may exist between brain states and mental states. The hoary question of causality is shelved for future invest-igators to grapple with. Admittedly, even this correlational ques-tion still has a long way to go before being answered convincingly. The strategy scientists have adopted is to build on the most solid knowledge we have about the brain. This means that the question has to be focused on particular kinds of mental processes. A broad approach, aimed at explaining conscious states in general, is just too ambitious at present. Although that broader question remains one of the ultimate aims of brain research, it will have to await a general account of brain function. Such an account, a kind of 'the-ory of everything' for neurobiology, is a goal that science has not yet even begun to approach.

This brings us back to the visual system, which at the present time is undoubtedly the best-understood system in the brain. As we have tried to show in this book, the past quarter of a century has seen enormous breakthroughs in our knowledge of the neu-roscience of visual processing. So much so that Nobel laureate Francis Crick and neurobiologist Christof Koch have argued that the best way forward for attacking the problem of consciousness is through research on the 'visual brain'. Crick and Koch encap-sulated the problem by posing the questions 'What is it about the brain systems mediating visual processing that makes their activ-ity conscious?' and 'What is it about the brain activity underlying visual processing that makes it conscious under some conditions but unconscious under others?'

Of course, much of the work on the details of the visual brain has come from work in animals, particularly monkeys. In fact the wiring diagram of the ventral stream was initially worked out in the monkey. But tracing pathways in the monkey brain is one thing, determining what the monkey experiences is quite another. Humans can describe what they experience, monkeys cannot. So how do we show that in monkeys, just as in humans, the ventral stream plays the key role in constructing their visual experience? It is certainly difficult, but it's not impossible.

There is a good recent example of how this can be done. It provides direct evidence that what a monkey reports perceiving is

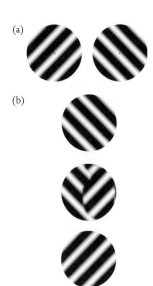

(a)

(b)

Figure 7.3

When incompatible images (a) are shown separately to our two eyes, we tend to alternate between seeing one and seeing the other (b, top and bottom). Rarely, but occasionally, do we see a composite of two images (as illustrated in b, middle). This so-called 'binocular rivalry' phenomenon has been used to study the neural correlates of visual consciousness.

directly related to neuronal activity in the highest regions of the ventral stream. As we saw in Chapter 4, neurons in the inferior temporal cortex of the monkey respond selectively to images like faces, colored shapes, and different kinds of objects. Nikos Logothetis and his colleagues in Germany have now shown that the activity of these neurons is closely linked to the perceptual experience of the monkey. They first trained the monkey to report, by pressing a lever, which of two alternative images it saw on a screen in front of it, over a period of 30 minutes or so. Sometimes one image would appear, say a picture of a face, sometimes the other, say a sunburst pattern; and whenever the picture changed, the monkey had to press the appropriate lever. Once the monkeys had learned this, the experimenters presented both images at once: one to each eye, causing 'binocular rivalry' (see Figure 7.3). When different incompatible images like this are simultaneously presented to the two eyes, a person almost never sees a fused combination of the two, but instead sees either the complete face or the complete sunburst pattern. It is as if the two pictures are competing with each other for consciousness. Sometimes you are conscious of one, sometimes the other: the two percepts alternate with each other at intervals of a few seconds or so. When the experimental animal was faced with binocular rivalry, it reported an alternating awareness of the two images just as a human would.

The exciting thing was that the responses of inferior temporal neurons followed the monkey's perceptual reports with a high correlation. Even though the images never changed physically on the screen, the monkey's reports of what it saw changed repeatedly; and these changes correlated with the fluctuating activity of neurons in its inferior temporal cortex. For example, a neuron that preferred faces responded strongly when the monkey reported seeing the face and weakly when it reported seeing the sunburst, and vice versa. But neurons earlier in the system, like area V1, did not show these correlations. They responded in the same way no matter what the monkey indicated that it saw. Even in intermediate areas such as V4, early in the ventral stream, the correlations were relatively weak.

It remains true that details of the brain are more easily studied in animals whereas the niceties of consciousness are more easily studied in humans. What is important is that whenever comparisons are made between the activity in visual areas in the monkey and the human, we see very similar things happening. This is perhaps unsurprising given the extent of our evolutionary heritage that humans share with monkeys. Nonetheless, it is important that findings like those of Logothetis be followed up in humans to see if the activity in our ventral stream also reflects our conscious visual experience. For obvious reasons it is difficult to look at the activity of single neurons in the human brain. But the advent of brain imaging techniques like functional magnetic resonance imaging makes it possible to measure the activity of large groups of neurons that share common visual properties. For example, as we saw in Chapter 5, Nancy Kanwisher and her colleagues used fMRI to delineate two ventral-stream areas, one called the fusiform face area (FFA), which is selectively activated by pictures of faces, and another area, the parahippocampal place area (PPA), which is activated mostly by pictures of houses or scenes. She used this difference between the two areas to study the changes in visual consciousness during binocular rivalry in much the same way as Logothetis had done in the monkey. Kanwisher, together with her colleague Frank Tong and others, scanned the brains of volunteers while showing them pictures of a face and a house simultaneously, one picture to each eye. Just like Logothetis's monkeys, sometimes the volunteers would see the house and sometimes the face, but almost never both at once. They were asked to press a key whenever one percept was replaced by the other. Whenever the volunteers reported seeing the face there was more activity in their FFA but when they reported seeing the house, there was more activity in their PPA. In other words, the activity in the FFA and the PPA reflected what they consciously perceived, not what was on their retina.

Tim Andrews, a neuroscientist at the University of Durham, has addressed the same kind of question, but using the ambiguous 'face/vase' figure shown in Figure 7.4. Just like our perception of the competing images in binocular rivalry, our perception of this ambiguous figure changes from moment to moment. Sometimes we see a vase on a dark background and sometimes we see two profile faces against a light background. But we never see both at once. Andrews took advantage of the fact that objects like the vase activate another area in the ventral stream, the lateral occipital area (LO: see Chapter 5), rather than the FFA. He presented volunteers

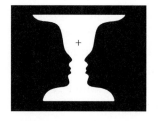

Figure 7.4

The famous face-vase picture, devised by Edgar Rubin, a Danish psychologist, is an example of an ambiguous figure. Sometimes we see two black faces against a white background, and sometimes we see a white vase against a black background. We cannot see both at once. This ambiguous figure, like binocular rivalry displays, has been used to study visual consciousness.

with the face/vase figure to look at for a few minutes, asking them to press a key every time they saw the faces change to a vase or vice-versa, and contrasted the activity in area LO with activity in the FFA. The results were clear. The changes in perception were closely correlated with activity changes between the FFA and area LO. In other words, although these observers were looking at an unchanging screen, their brain activity kept switching between the FFA and area LO. And when it did, what they 'saw' changed as well.

In summary, we have converging evidence from three kinds of research that allows us to be rather confident that neural activity in the ventral stream is closely correlated with visual consciousness. First, we have lesion evidence: this shows us that the ventral stream is a necessary part of the circuitry for visual awareness. Without the ventral stream, there is no visual consciousness. Second, we know from fMRI evidence that fluctuations in visual awareness are closely correlated with changes in the activation of different areas within the ventral stream. And third, we have evidence from single neuron recordings in monkeys that the activity of cells in inferotemporal cortex is tightly linked to perceptual fluctuations. While this evidence is indirect in that we can only assume that the monkey's visual experience resembles our own, nonetheless studies of this kind provide our first real handle on what may be happening at the level of individual neurons. Together, these three lines of inquiry give us a convincing lead on where in the brain neuronal activity correlates with visual awareness. But of course they do not explain what it is about the neurons in the ventral stream that gives them this property.

After all, none of these studies shows that ventral stream activation is *always* associated with awareness. On the contrary, they show quite the opposite. Consider the fate of the stimulus that temporarily lost the competition in the fMRI studies. Not only did they still activate earlier areas of the visual cortex like V1, but they also activated to some extent the relevant ventral-stream areas (FFA, PPA or area LO). In other words, in these studies, the activation went up or down according to whether the stimulus was conscious or unconscious, but it never actually disappeared altogether. So why is ventral-stream activity sometimes conscious and sometimes unconscious? It could, of course, be that the sheer amount of activity in a particular ventral stream area determines whether or not its activity leads to a conscious experience. Alternatively, it could be that the activity in that area has to be synchronized with activity elsewhere in the brain, either earlier visual areas like V1, and/or higher-order structures such as the frontal lobes. There is a lot of speculation about such possibilities, but to date there is a shortage of convincing empirical evidence to support any particular hypothesis.

So we have no real idea what the critical difference is between neural activity that reaches awareness and that which does not. But certainly visual information that does not reach awareness does get processed to quite a high level of analysis in the ventral stream. This processing could well account for so-called unconscious perception, in which subliminal (subjectively unseen) stimuli can influence behavior. For example, seeing a subliminal image of a cat can speed up your reaction to a semantically related image, like a dog, that you are being asked to classify with a quick key-press. But what should be emphasized here is that although unconscious perception does seem to occur, it arises from activity within the ventral, not the dorsal stream. In fact, the visual computations underlying unconscious perception seem to be identical to those underlying conscious perception: it's just that they don't make it into awareness.

But what about visually elicited activity in the dorsal stream? This activity certainly does not give rise to visual awareness either, but that doesn't mean that it has anything to do with unconscious perception. Use of that phrase carries an implication that such visual processing could, in principle, be conscious. The fact is that visual activity in the dorsal stream can never become conscious— so 'perception' is the wrong word to use. The dorsal stream is not in the business of providing any kind of a visual representation of the world: it just converts visual information directly into action. The visual processing that it carries out is no more accessible to conscious scrutiny than the visual processing that elicits the pupillary light reflex. Dorsal stream processing is more complex than that which supports the pupillary light reflex, but in the end they are both simply visuomotor control systems with no more pretensions to consciousness than we see in the robot in a tele-assistance network. It is the human operator (the ventral stream) that provides the conscious monitoring of what's going on, even though it is the robot (the dorsal stream) that is doing the work.

Summary

We have tried in this book to make a strong case for the idea that vision is not unitary, and that our visual phenomenology reflects only one aspect of what the visual brain is doing. Much of what vision does for us lies outside our visual experience. Indeed, most of our actions are controlled by essentially robotic systems that use visual computations that are completely inaccessible to conscious scrutiny. This might sound rather like Cartesian dualism—the existence of a conscious mind separate from a reflexive machine. But the separation we are suggesting has nothing to do with the kind of dualism that Descartes proposed. Although the two kinds of visual processing are separate, both are embodied in the hardware of the brain. Moreover, as we have tried to show in this chapter, there is a complex but seamless interaction between the ventral perception stream and the dorsal action stream in the production of adaptive behavior.

8

Postscript: Dee's life fifteen years on

If you were a visitor at Dee's home today, you would find it hard to believe that she had any visual problems at all. She would welcome you at the door, invite you in, and no doubt show you around the now fully renovated house, including Carlo's wine cellar (converted from an original seventeenth-century structure), his pride and joy. She would almost certainly give you a guided tour of her garden—which is her pride and joy. She would walk you confidently down the path, pausing here and there to point out a particularly beautiful plant or flowering shrub. A little later, in the kitchen, as she made you a cup of tea, you would again see little sign of the devastating loss of form perception that we described earlier in this book. She would have no problem putting the kettle on the stove, finding the tea, milk and sugar, and pouring the boiling water into the teapot. She would need no help in bringing the tray out to the terrace, where she would pour you a cup of tea. In fact, Dee in all these activities behaves so naturally and ably that you would never suspect that she had ever suffered the devastating loss of sight that she did. Of course she could *always* do much more than her conscious sight would seem to allow, even from early on. But her repertoire of visual skills has improved by leaps and bounds over the fifteen years since her accident. Her self-confidence and sureness of touch have increased steadily, hand in hand with these developing skills.

It is an important research question in itself to work out how it is that anyone who has suffered major brain damage can show such dramatic improvements over the years. Of course, some of the things that Dee can do are fairly easily explained. According to our 'two visual systems' account, Dee has a well-functioning visuomotor system. Using this system, she can still use vision to negotiate her way through a garden replete with paths and flowerbeds and to guide hand movements like picking up the kettle or handing you a teacup. But although this explains how she picks up the kettle, it doesn't explain how she selected the kettle in the first place. It also doesn't explain why she is so much better at everyday tasks now than she was fifteen years ago, right after the accident.

One of the ways Dee can do this is not at all mysterious. Just like any person whose vision suddenly becomes impaired, she makes life easier for herself by making sure that things in the kitchen and around the rest of the house are kept in the same place from day to day. In conjunction with this commonsense strategy, she has the advantage over a blind person that she can guide her movements accurately to such objects without having to depend on memory and touch. She can do much more than this, however. For example, she can choose between two or more objects that happen to be on the counter—picking up the teacup instead of the coffee mug, for example. It helps a great deal that many things in the world have distinctive colors—and Dee still has vivid color perception. She has no trouble identifying flowers— and even foliage—by subtle differences in their color and visual texture. The same is true of many manufactured objects in the kitchen and tool shed, which again often have distinctive colors and sheens.

But Dee has other ways of telling things apart that are not so obvious to the observer or even to her. We accidentally encountered an example of these more subtle strategies when testing her in the laboratory several years ago, using our usual 'Efron blocks'. In the particular experiment we were doing, she was asked to reach out and pick up a square block presented alongside a rectangular one of the same overall area (or vice versa). We didn't expect her to be able to do this. After all, she couldn't consciously distinguish between the two blocks. To our surprise, she reached out and picked up the right one much more often than she could have done by simply guessing. How did she know which one to pick up, when in other tests she couldn't tell us which was which? The secret was revealed when we noticed that she sometimes reached toward the wrong block but then corrected herself in midstream. When we examined videotapes of her movements, we discovered that this self-correction happened quite often—and when it did she was almost always correct on that trial. In fact, when we examined only those trials where she went straight for one of the blocks, her performance fell to chance. So what was going on here? We think she must have been somehow monitoring the posture of her hand as she reached out toward one of the blocks. If it didn't 'feel' right she simply switched mid-flight to the other block. In other words, she was using feedback from her own finger movements to tell her whether the object she was heading for was the correct one. Having calibrated the action using her visuomotor system, which was able to compute the width of the object, she could use feedback from her action to help her make the correct choice. Dee wasn't deliberately cheating; she was just doing what she had to do to solve the task. She probably just experienced it as the everyday feeling we all have of sometimes changing our mind between two alternative courses of action.

If Dee could pull this kind of 'trick' in the laboratory, then it seems likely that she was doing the same thing all the time in her everyday life. In fact, we got the impression—since she used the trick right from the start of the test session—that she had already learned, albeit unconsciously, that monitoring her own movements was a useful strategy. This kind of learning must have been happening almost as soon as Dee started to deal with her impoverished visual world. Such behavioral compensation is a natural way of dealing with the problems faced by any brain-damaged person: you do whatever you can to solve the problems that face you. You may not know how you are doing it, but if it works you adopt it. In fact, later on, Dee seems to have taken these behavioral aids a step further by internalizing the whole thing, so that she didn't even need to perform an action explicitly. She became able to cue herself just by *imagining* performing a particular action on the object in front of her, without actually doing it.

Our evidence for this internalization of Dee's self-monitoring strategy came from a study in which we asked her to show us the slant of a line drawn on a piece of paper by copying the line on a separate piece of paper. In theory she once more shouldn't have been able to do this: after all, it was just like asking her to match the orientation of a slot by rotating a card held in her hand. As we described early on in this book, she was quite unable to do that— at least, not at first. But we didn't mention then that it didn't take her long to learn a trick to deal with the slot-matching task—one that worked in much the same way as the self-correction ploy in the block-grasping task we have just described. What Dee did was to surreptitiously 'break the rules' and move the card a little way toward the slot as if she were about to mail it, rather than holding it in place and just rotating it. Presumably she was engaging her visuomotor system by making this incipient posting movement. This way, she could line up the card with the orientation of the slot—and then hold it at that angle to offer her 'perceptual report' of the slot. Again, it was not an attempt to cheat: like all of us, Dee wanted to do well, and this was how she could best solve the task she was given, which was to match the card to the orientation of the slot. In one sense that was a perfectly valid of performing the task we gave her; it is just that the most natural way for most of us to do the task would be to use something Dee could not use: our visual experience of what the slot actually looks like.

So we should have guessed that Dee would adopt a similar sort of strategy, if she could, when asked to copy lines. And of course she did, at least until we told her not to. What she did was to 'trace' a line in the air above each line we showed her, and then make the same movement on the paper with the pencil. So her drawings were much more accurate than they should have been. But even when Dee agreed to stop tracing in the air, she continued to draw her lines far better than chance. In struggling to understand this, we noticed that her drawing movements still didn't look like normal copying. Dee would look fixedly at the original line for a few seconds each time, with her pencil on the other piece of paper, before then quickly drawing her line. Afterwards she confessed how she was doing it. Instead of explicitly tracing in the air over the top of the line, she *imagined* doing that, while keeping her pencil on the paper. She then drew her line quickly, before the imagined movement had faded from her mind. Since this ploy seemed to take Dee a few seconds, we thought that if we asked her to copy the line as soon as we presented it to her, she wouldn't have time to generate an imagined movement. The result was dramatic: Dee's lines were now random, and they showed no systematic relationship to the line she was shown. All she could now do was to guess. Only when she had time to imagine making a tracing movement was she able to draw a line that matched the original.

In all of these fascinating strategies, Dee was not so much telling us about what she could *see*, but rather about what she could *do*. In other words, she was using her intact visuomotor system in the dorsal stream, not to improve her perception, but rather as an *alternative* to perception, which allowed her to give the right answers to the problems we had presented her with. She was solving a problem that was designed to test perception without using perception at all.

There is a lesson here, which is recognized by all experienced clinicians who routinely test patients with brain damage. The fact that a patient passes a test doesn't mean that the patient is doing so in the way that the designer of the test intended. As the old saying goes, 'there's more than one way to skin a cat.' It is a natural and highly beneficial tendency of humans (and other animals) that if they cannot solve a problem in the most obvious way, they will try to solve it in other, less obvious, ways. This indeed is one of the major foundations of neurological rehabilitation: the therapist tries to find an alternative route by which the patient's deficits can be circumvented. Often these require specific training, but in many other cases, particularly over periods of years, patients will come up with such strategies themselves. Dee is a good example of this.

To deal with everyday problems that would normally require perception of the form and shape of objects, Dee has to rely on strategies like those we have outlined above because her brain damage has completely devastated the ventral stream pathways that process form. As mentioned in Chapter 5, we have obtained objective confirmation of this ventral stream damage from recent brain imaging studies in collaboration with Tom James and Jody Culham at the University of Western Ontario, using the powerful 4-Tesla magnet located at the Robarts Research Institute there. These studies have allowed us to look in more detail than was previously possible at the actual workings of Dee's visual system, and not only at its structure. We carried out a systematic series of brain scans, requiring Dee to spend time inside the magnet not just once but for several scanning sessions. This was not easy for her because it meant she had to keep completely still in the confined space within the bore of the magnet for more than thirty minutes at a time. Not only is the inside of the magnet dark and oppressive, particularly for someone like Dee who is already a bit claustrophobic, but it is extremely noisy as well. Nevertheless, Dee persevered and overcame her reluctance with real fortitude, and we were able to obtain some excellent images of her brain.

We started by carrying out an accurate structural scan of her brain, and then used functional imaging to try to identify which visual areas were still working, and which areas had been destroyed. First we looked for area LO, which as we saw in Chapter 5 is an area in the ventral stream that is specifically activated when a person looks at objects, or even at line drawings or pictures of objects. Of course, whenever we look at a picture of an object, widespread brain activity is produced. Early visual areas that are sensitive to lines and color, for example, will be activated if lines and color are present in the picture. To exclude these areas from the functional image we have to use the subtraction method described in Plate 8 (top). In this study, what we did was to contrast the pattern of brain activation that occurred when subjects (including both Dee and healthy volunteers) looked at pictures of real objects with the activation that occurred when they looked at scrambled versions of those same pictures. The difference between the brain activity generated by these two different sets of pictures should reveal the areas specific for processing real objects, and in the case of Dee, whether or not the pattern of activations is normal.

Not surprisingly, the brains of our healthy volunteers showed a robust activation in area LO. This area of activation corresponded remarkably well with the location of the damaged area in Dee's brain (Plate 7, top). The correspondence became even more evident when the activation in a control subject's brain was mathematically superimposed onto a section through Dee's brain (Plate 7, bottom right). This activity fell neatly within the areas of lost tissue on both sides of her brain. In confirmation of that, when we looked at the pattern of activation in Dee's brain using the same subtraction method, the functional images showed no different activation for line drawings of objects than they did for scrambled versions (Plate 7, bottom left). Just as we had inferred from our original testing many years ago, her brain registers the presence of lines and edges at early levels of the visual system, but it cannot put these elements together to form perceived 'wholes', due to the damage in her ventral stream.

As we already knew, however, Dee can recognize objects on the basis of their color and visual texture. We were not too surprised therefore to find that colored photographs of objects produced quite a bit of activation in Dee's brain as compared with scrambled versions of the same colored photographs. This activation was not in area LO (which of course was badly damaged) but was located instead in neighboring regions of the ventral stream. Similar regions were activated to some extent in our healthy volunteers, although there was much more activation in area LO. It is possible that the activated regions outside area LO in Dee represent processing that is related not to objects per se but to the surfaces that make up objects. This would explain how Dee continues to perceive the color and other surface properties of objects, despite being unable to perceive the object that these surfaces define. It is also possible, however, that these areas are being recruited in Dee's brain to do things that they do not normally do in the healthy brain.

A completely different story emerged when we looked at brain activation in Dee's dorsal stream. For the first time, we examined not the parts of her visual brain that we assumed were damaged, but instead the parts that seemed to be working well. We used Jody Culham's 'grasparatus' (see Plate 8, bottom) to identify which areas of Dee's brain became active when she reached out and grasped small blocks presented to her in the magnet—and how these areas corresponded to those that were active in the brains of healthy volunteers when doing the same task. The results nicely confirmed our earlier speculations—that is, we found that just as in our normal volunteers, Dee's brain showed activation in area AIP at the anterior end of the intraparietal sulcus. As we noted in earlier chapters, this part of the human dorsal stream appears to correspond closely to the similarly located area AIP in the monkey, which is known to be intimately associated with the visual control of grasping.

These brain imaging studies, by providing both a confirmation and a clarification of what we had inferred on the basis of behavioral testing, illustrate the value of systematic neuropsychological investigations of patients with brain damage. In Dee's case, her pattern of impaired and intact visual abilities maps beautifully onto the patterns of brain activation in her ventral and dorsal streams as revealed by brain imaging. Taken together, the totality of our findings with Dee reflect not so much a recovery of damaged brain function, so much as her learning to exploit intact brain structures, in particular those in her dorsal stream. In this way, she is able to cope with the challenges facing her as she tries to live as full a life as possible within her diminished visual world. In short, her brain has adapted to the loss of one of its major components by a large-scale reorganization of how it controls itself. Rather like an ice hockey team that has lost a player because of penalties, the damaged brain has to adapt and form a new dynamic configuration. Like the team, if the brain does this, it can still perform well enough to cope successfully with many of the challenges it faces.

The story could have been very different if Dee had sustained her brain damage early in life, before puberty, while her brain was still developing and still retained a degree of plasticity. In such cases, the damage can often be bypassed, by co-opting pathways normally used by the brain for other purposes altogether. Unfortunately for Dee, she suffered her brain damage in adulthood. In contrast, another patient with visual form agnosia we have been studying recently, Serge Blanc, suffered his very extensive brain damage as a result of a brain infection at age three. Although he, like Dee, has enormous difficulties in recognizing shapes and patterns, he does have some conscious perception of the simple features of the pictures we show him. Sometimes he can painstakingly put these together and infer what it is he is looking at. Dee cannot do this. Functional imaging studies by Jean-François Démonet and Sandra Lê at Toulouse in France, suggest that Serge achieves this perception of simple lines and edges by redeploying parts of his parietal cortex as an alternative to his totally destroyed ventral stream.

Although the young developing brain has much greater ability to rewire itself than the mature brain, we now know that some limited rewiring can occur in the adult brain. The challenge is to work out how this happens and how it can be encouraged to happen even more. Introducing human stem cells (the developmental precursors of all kinds of cells, including neurons) into damaged areas of the brain is one promising way ahead for scientists to explore how new brain circuits can be encouraged to replace the missing ones. Another promising avenue is the use of the brain's own chemicals to promote the growth of new connections and pathways in the human brain. All of this lies in the future, but there is real scope for optimism that within a few years the kinds of brain damage we have seen in Dee would not be irreversible, and that people like her could once again come to see the world with the full richness that the rest of us normally take for granted.

Summary

Although Dee has learned to cope with her visual disabilities remarkably well, careful behavioral testing reveals that her damaged perceptual system has shown little recovery in the fifteen years since her accident. She has learned to use visuomotor tricks to compensate for the absence of form perception, but her object recognition deficits are still apparent when we take care to prevent her from using these various coping strategies. Recent anatomical and functional MRIs of her brain have provided powerful confirmation of the conclusions we drew from our earlier behavioral work with Dee. In fact, the neuroimaging evidence could not be more clear: Dee's ventral stream is severely damaged, but her dorsal stream appears to be working relatively normally. However, the functional neuroimaging evidence is also giving us new information that goes well beyond our earlier speculations. For example, we are finding significant activation of certain areas within the ventral stream that have not been lost—presumably either because information is getting through along essentially normal routes, or because new routes have opened up. Further investigation of these patterns of activation, and how they change when Dee views different pictures and scenes, promise to reveal new insights into the ventral stream's normal modus operandi, as well as information about the brain areas that are called into service when she engages in new strategies to get around her impairments. The remarkable visuomotor adaptations that Dee has acquired over the years provide a powerful testimony to the robustness of the human condition. Studying the way the brain reorganizes itself in response to severe damage presents one of the most important challenges to neuroscience in the twenty-first century.

Epilogue

Our understanding of how each of the two streams contributes to behavior is advancing rapidly. These advances are benefiting from converging research from a growing range of different approaches, all of which are becoming progressively more sophisticated and powerful. When we began to study Dee Fletcher in St Andrews back in 1988, functional MRI was unknown, and the high-resolution measurement of human movement had scarcely begun. Now we are witnessing further refinements of these technologies and methodologies, and seeing complementary ones emerging, for example transcranial magnetic stimulation (TMS), a procedure in which a small area of the brain of a healthy volunteer can be briefly but reversibly disabled at particular points during performance of some behavioral or perceptual task. In addition, advances in molecular neurobiology and genetics are being applied to the study of how the brain controls behavior, particularly learning and memory. For example, it is now possible to see what genes are 'turned on' in different parts of the brain during the learning of new skills, including visually guided ones.

The research we have surveyed in this book provides an example of how different complementary scientific approaches to understanding the brain can converge together to provide powerful insights. No one method alone could have come up with such a convincing story of how the brain's visual system works. Indeed, the progress that has been made underscores the utility of such multidisciplinary approaches to the study of brain and behavior.

Until now, the emphasis in much of the work has been on the differences between the two visual streams in the cerebral cortex— establishing where they go, why they are there, and how they work. This side of the story has depended crucially on evidence from patients like Dee who have suffered damage to one or the other stream. In the future the most exciting advances are likely to come from applying new investigative methods to the task of learning how the two streams work, not just in isolation but together, in all of the different aspects of our visual life.

It is impossible to predict how the technology available to human neuroscience will develop over the coming years. It seems likely, however, that increasingly refined noninvasive stimulation and recording methods will come into use. Already investigators are devising ways of combining TMS and fMRI technology in simultaneous brain stimulation and imaging experiments. As the precision and sophistication of the tools available to us improve, their combined use promises to reveal even more insights into how the brain works. The advances over the next 15 years are likely to be even more revolutionary than those we have seen over the last fifteen.

Further Reading

Chapter 1. A tragic accident

An English translation of Lissauer's classic paper on visual agnosia is provided by:

Shallice, T., & Jackson, M. (1988). Lissauer on agnosia. *Cognitive Neuropsychology*, 5, 153–92. (translation of: Lissauer, H. (1890). A case of visual agnosia with a contribution to theory)

For an up-to-date review of the varieties of visual agnosias, see:

Farah, M.J. (2004). *Visual agnosia (2nd Edition)*. Cambridge MA: MIT Press/Bradford Books.

There are two classic papers on Mr. S., a patient who also experienced a hypoxic episode from carbon monoxide inhalation, and whose resulting deficits were remarkably similar to Dee's:

Benson, D.F. and Greenberg, J.P. (1969). Visual form agnosia: A specific deficit in visual discrimination. *Archives of Neurology*, 20, 82–9.

Efron, R. (1969). What is perception? *Boston Studies in the Philosophy of Science*, 4, 137–73.

Chapter 2: Doing without seeing

These two early publications describe Dee's spared visual abilities and deficits in detail:

Milner, A.D., Perrett, D.I., Johnston, R.S., Benson, P.J., Jordan, T.R., Heeley, D.W., Bettucci, D., Mortara, F., Mutani, R., Terazzi, E., and Davidson, D.L.W. (1991). Perception and action in 'visual form agnosia'. *Brain*, 114, 405–28.

Goodale, M.A., Milner, A.D., Jakobson, L.S., and Carey, D.P. (1991). A neurological dissociation between perceiving objects and grasping them. *Nature*, 349, 154–6.

For a classic account of seminal work on the visual control of action by a pioneer in the field, see:

Jeannerod, M. (1986). Mechanisms of visuomotor coordination: a study in normal and brain-damaged subjects. *Neuropsychologia*, 24, 41–78.

Chapter 3: When vision for action fails

The first description of optic ataxia is given in this classic paper by Rudolph Bálint, translated by Monika Harvey:

Harvey, M. (1995). Translation of 'Psychic paralysis of gaze, optic ataxia, and spatial disorder of attention' by Rudolph Bálint. *Cognitive Neuropsychology*, 12, 261–82.

The true nature of optic ataxia began to become clear with the publication of the following paper nearly 80 years after Bálint's original case report:

Perenin, M.-T. and Vighetto, A. (1988). Optic ataxia: a specific disruption in visuomotor mechanisms. I. Different aspects of the deficit in reaching for objects. *Brain*, 111, 643–74.

This book provides a comprehensive review of work on the neural substrates of the visually guided action, including descriptions of the reaching and grasping deficits in optic ataxia:

Jeannerod, M. (1997). *The cognitive neuroscience of action*. Oxford: Blackwell.

Chapter 4: The origins of vision: From modules to models

David Ingle provided a compelling demonstration of the existence of parallel but independent visuomotor systems in a lower vertebrate in the following paper:

Ingle, D. (1973). Two visual systems in the frog. *Science*, 181, 1053–55.

The evolution of brains is discussed (and beautifully illustrated) in the following book:

Allman, J.M. (1999). *Evolving brains*. New York: Scientific American Library.

This book by Semir Zeki provides a wonderful, if idiosyncratic, account of the physiology and anatomy of the primate visual system:

Zeki, S. (1993). *A vision of the brain*. Oxford: Blackwell Scientific Publications.

The following articles provide more detailed accounts of recent work on the monkey ventral and dorsal streams, respectively:

Tanaka, K. (1996). Inferotemporal cortex and object vision. *Annual Review of Neuroscience*, 19, 109–39.

Andersen, R.A. and Buneo, C.A. (2003). Sensorimotor integration in posterior parietal cortex. *Advances in Neurology*, 93, 159–77.

For a detailed account of the division of labor between the dorsal and ventral streams, readers might wish to consult our earlier book:

Milner, A.D. and Goodale, M.A. (1995). *The visual brain in action*. Oxford: Oxford University Press.

A short précis of *The Visual Brain in Action* can be found at the following website: http://psyche.cs.monash.edu.au/v4/psyche-4-12-milner.html

Chapter 5: Streams within streams

The recent book by Martha Farah (see readings for Chapter 1) provides an excellent overview of the higher-level deficits in perception that can follow damage to the ventral stream and other brain areas.

This edited collection of case studies further illustrates the broad range of selective deficits in perception that have been described in the neurological and neuropsychological literature:

Humphreys, G.W. (2001). *Case studies in the neuropsychology of vision.* London: Psychology Press.

The following paper by Morris Moscovitch and colleagues describes Charles K., a man with visual object agnosia but intact imagery and face recognition:

Moscovitch, M., Winocur, G., and Behrmann, M. (1997). What is special about face recognition? Nineteen experiments on a person with visual object agnosia and dyslexia but normal face recognition. *Journal of Cognitive Neuroscience,* 9, 555–604.

For a discussion of face perception in general, see:

Bruce, V. and Young, A.W. (1998): *In the eye of the beholder: the science of face perception.* Oxford: Oxford University Press.

The three papers below provide reviews of the functional organization of the human dorsal and ventral streams as revealed by functional MRI:

Culham, J.C. and Kanwisher, N.G. (2001). Neuroimaging of cognitive functions in human parietal cortex. *Current Opinion in Neurobiology,* 11, 157–63.

Grill-Spector, K. (2003). The neural basis of object perception. *Current Opinion in Neurobiology,* 13, 159–66.

Malach, R., Levy, I., and Hasson, U. (2002). The topography of high-order human object areas. *Trends in Cognitive Sciences,* 6, 176–84.

For readers who would like to know more about how functional MRI can be used to study a range of psychological phenomena, the following book provides an excellent overview:

Huettel, S.A., Song, A.W., and McCarthy, G. (2004). *Functional magnetic resonance imaging.* Sunderland, MA: Sinauer Associates.

These two books by Larry Weiskrantz offer an authoritative account of blindsight and related disorders by a pioneer in the field:

Weiskrantz, L. (1990): *Blindsight: a case study and implications.* Oxford: Oxford University Press.

Weiskrantz, L. (1997): *Consciousness lost and found: a neuropsychological exploration.* Oxford: Oxford University Press.

Chapter 6: Why do we need two systems?

The late Keith Humphrey was instrumental in showing how the distinction between vision for perception and vision for action could help bridge the gap between previous theoretical accounts by individuals like James J. Gibson, David Marr, Richard Gregory, and Ulrich Neisser. Some of these ideas are set out in the following paper:

Goodale, M.A. and Humphrey, G.K. (1998). The objects of action and perception. *Cognition*, 67, 181–207.

For a discussion of 'change blindness' and its implications for understanding our everyday visual experience, see:

Rensink, R.A. (2001). Change Blindness: Implications for the Nature of Attention. In MR Jenkin and LR Harris (eds.), *Vision and Attention* (pp. 169–188). New York: Springer.

The following reviews examine the evidence that many of our actions are immune to pictorial illusions:

Goodale, M.A. and Westwood, D.A. (2004). An evolving view of duplex vision: separate but interacting cortical pathways for perception and action. *Current Opinion in Neurobiology*, 14, 203–11.

Goodale, M.A., Westwood, D.A., and Milner, A.D. (2004). Two distinct modes of control for object-directed action. *Progress in Brain Research*, 144, 131–44.

Milner, A.D. and Dyde, R.T. (2003). Why do some perceptual illusions affect visually guided action, when others don't? *Trends in Cognitive Science*, 7, 10–11.

For an excellent introduction to the psychology of perception, including the perceptual constancies, the reader might wish to consult:

Gregory, R.L. (1997). *Eye and Brain, 5th Edition* Oxford: Oxford University Press.

Chapter 7: Getting it all together

Feedback as well as feedforward neural connections are likely to play a crucial role in the integration of activity in the two visual streams. For an interesting account of the possible role of feedback connections in visual processing, see:

Lamme, V.A. and Roelfsema, P.R. (2000). The distinct modes of vision offered by feedforward and recurrent processing. *Trends in Neurosciences*, 23, 571–9.

This article shows how areas in the dorsal stream that are closely linked to the control of eye movements also play an important role in the shifting of attention from one object to another:

Colby, C.L. and Goldberg, M.E. (1999). Space and attention in parietal cortex. *Annual Review of Neuroscience*, 22, 319–49.

In this paper, the authors review evidence showing how perceptual information from the ventral stream is integrated with information processed by the dorsal stream in the production of skilled motor acts:
Goodale, M.A. and Haffenden, A.M. (2003). Interactions between the dorsal and ventral streams of visual processing. *Advances in Neurology*, 93, 249–67.

The late Nobel Laureate, Francis Crick, devoted the latter part of his scientific career to pursuing the neural basis of consciousness. A flavor of his approach to the problem can be gleaned from the following article that he wrote with his long-time collaborator Christof Koch:
Crick, F. and Koch, C. (2003). A framework for consciousness. *Nature Neuroscience*, 6, 119–126.

Christof Koch has also written a highly accessible discussion of these ideas in a recent book:
Koch, C. (2003). *The quest for consciousness: a neurobiological approach.* California: Roberts and Company.

The following paper shows how empirical methods can be used to study the neural correlates of perceptual experience in the monkey. Using a combination of a clever behavioral paradigm along with single-neuron recording techniques, Nikos Logothetis was able to show that neural activity in high-level areas of the ventral stream is related directly to visual awareness:
Logothetis, N.K. (1998). Single units and conscious vision. *Philosophical Transactions of the Royal Society of London B: Biological Sciences*, 353, 1801–18.

One of the most influential philosophers writing about the nature of consciousness is David Chalmers. The following two papers give a good indication of his ideas:
Chalmers, D.J. (1995). Facing up to the problem of consciousness. *Journal of Consciousness Studies*, 2, 200–19.
Chalmers, D.J. (2004). How can we construct a science of consciousness? In M.S. Gazzaniga (ed.): The Cognitive Neurosciences III. Cambridge, MA: MIT Press.

Chapter 8: Postscript: Dee's life 15 years on

Our discoveries of some of Dee's strategies for dealing with perceptual tasks are detailed in these two papers:
Murphy, K. J., Racicot, C. I., and Goodale, M.A. (1996). The use of visuomotor cues as a strategy for making perceptual judgements in a patient with visual form agnosia. *Neuropsychology*, 10, 396–401.
Dijkerman, H.C. and Milner, A.D. (1997). Copying without perceiving: motor imagery in visual form agnosia. *Neuroreport*, 8, 729–32.

Our initial neuroimaging study of the damaged and functionally intact brain systems in Dee's brain is described in the following paper:

James, T.W., Culham, J., Humphrey, G.K., Milner, A.D., and Goodale, M.A. (2003). Ventral occipital lesions impair object recognition but not object-directed grasping: An fMRI study. *Brain*, 126, 2463–75.

In further work, we have found that Dee's spared perception of colour and texture allows her to distinguish between scenes like beaches, forests, cityscapes, etc. This information appears to be sufficient to activate her parahippocampal place area, which has survived the damage to her ventral stream:

Steeves, J.K., Humphrey, G.K., Culham, J.C., Menon, R.S., Milner, A.D. and Goodale, M.A. (2004). Behavioral and neuroimaging evidence for a contribution of color and texture information to scene classification in a patient with visual form agnosia. *Journal of Cognitive Neuroscience*, 16, 955–65.

This paper provides a description of 'Serge Blanc', the second patient with visual form agnosia we have been able to study in some detail, and who differs from Dee in having had almost all of his life to adjust to his visual deficits:

Lê, S., Cardebat, D., Boulanouar, K., Hénaff, M.A., Michel, F., Milner, A.D., Dijkerman, H.C., Puel, M., Démonet, J.F. (2002). Seeing, since childhood, without ventral stream: a behavioural study. *Brain*, 125, 58–74.

For a convincing account of how experience can shape our brain—and how experience can be manipulated to rehabilitate individuals with brain damage, see:

Robertson, I.H. (1999): *Mind sculpture: unlocking your brain's untapped potential*. New York: Fromm International.

INDEX

Note: 'f' after a page number indicates a reference to a figure, 't' indicates a reference to a table.

Index